BRITISH COASTAL WEAPONS
VS
GERMAN COASTAL WEAPONS

The Dover Strait 1940–44

NEIL SHORT

OSPREY PUBLISHING
Bloomsbury Publishing Plc
Kemp House, Chawley Park, Cumnor Hill, Oxford OX2 9PH, UK
29 Earlsfort Terrace, Dublin 2, Ireland
1385 Broadway, 5th Floor, New York, NY 10018, USA
E-mail: info@ospreypublishing.com
www.ospreypublishing.com

OSPREY is a trademark of Osprey Publishing Ltd

First published in Great Britain in 2023

A catalogue record for this book is available from the British Library.

ISBN: PB 9781472849779; eBook 9781472849793; ePDF 9781472849762;
XML 9781472849786

23 24 25 26 27   10 9 8 7 6 5 4 3 2 1

Colour artworks by Adam Hook
Maps by Bounford.com
Index by Alison Worthington
Typeset by PDQ Digital Media Solutions, Bungay, UK
Printed and bound in India by Replika Press Private Ltd.

Artist's note
Readers may care to note that the original paintings from which the colour
plates in this book were prepared are available for private sale. All reproduction
copyright whatsoever is retained by the publishers. All enquiries should be
addressed to:

Scorpio, 158 Mill Road, Hailsham, East Sussex BN27 2SH, UK
Email: scorpiopaintings@btinternet.com

The publishers regret that they can enter into no correspondence upon this
matter.

Osprey Publishing supports the Woodland Trust, the UK's leading woodland
conservation charity.

To find out more about our authors and books visit
www.ospreypublishing.com. Here you will find extracts, author interviews,
details of forthcoming events and the option to sign up for our newsletter.

Author's acknowledgements
I am indebted to a number of people and organizations in the production of
this book. In particular, I would like to thank the staff and members of the
Kent Archives, Dover Museum, above all Dr Lynda Pearce and Jon Iveson, St
Margaret's History Society, the Kent Archaeological Society and the Royal
Artillery Museum, especially Siân Mogridge. I would also like to express my
thanks to the staff and volunteers of the National Trust, especially Jon Barker,
Robert Hall and a special mention to Gordon Wise who showed me around
the British gun positions, answered my many questions and kindly read the
manuscript. I would also like to thank John Guy who was generous with his
extensive knowledge of the British and German guns. I have endeavoured to
corral all the facts clearly and accurately, but where I have fallen short the
responsibility is all mine. Finally, I would like to thank my family – Nikki,
Amy and Lewis. Despite the difficulties of the pandemic, they supported me
on trips to Kent, the archives and eventually to France. Hopefully the sacrifices
were worthwhile.

A note on measure
Both Imperial and metric measurements have been used in this book. A
conversion table is provided below:
1in. = 2.54cm
1ft = 0.3m
1yd = 0.9m
1 mile = 1.6km
1lb = 0.45kg
1 long ton = 1.02 metric tonnes

1mm = 0.039in.
1cm = 0.39in.
1m = 1.09yd
1km = 0.62 miles
1kg = 2.2lb
1 metric tonne = 0.98 long tons

Title page photograph: The 15in. guns of the British Wanstone Battery
firing in September 1944. (Library and Archives Canada/Department of
National Defence, e010786328)
Front cover, above: 'Jane', one of the 15in. guns at Wanstone Battery, is
shown firing. (Adam Hook)
Front cover, below: German K12 railway gun located at Stützpunkt 192
'Bismarck'. (Adam Hook)

CONTENTS

INTRODUCTION

In August 1940, the Germans fired their first shell across the English Channel. Soon after, the British responded. This was the initial exchange in a duel that was to last more than four years. Although the backdrop was bucolic – green fields, sandy beaches and of course the White Cliffs – the shelling was not dissimilar to that on the Western Front in World War I a quarter of a century earlier. Massive guns, both fixed and on rail carriages, fired thousands of shells, causing untold damage and killing countless civilians, sailors and soldiers. The violent exchanges were punctuated with long periods of relative peace, much as there had been on the Western Front. The Channel, normally a bustling trade route, was increasingly transformed into a no-go zone as the number of guns increased and the ability of both sides to identify and engage targets improved; eventually, shipping could be targeted even in bad weather and at night as both sides adopted radar.

At the start of the duel, in the summer of 1940, the greatest threat to the British Isles came not from coastal batteries, but from the air. The Luftwaffe attacked shipping in the Channel and the ports – the so-called *Kanalkampf*. Later, RAF airfields and radar stations were targeted as Hermann Göring sought to secure aerial supremacy, essential if a seaborne invasion of the British Isles was to be successful. In occupied Europe preparations for the invasion of Britain – *Unternehmen Seelöwe* (Operation *Sea Lion*) – were gaining momentum. Vessels were adapted for beach landings, troops trained and specialist weapons developed. The Luftwaffe, as it had in Poland and the West, would support the ground forces, but additionally the Germans installed large-calibre guns around Calais. These guns would be used to dominate the Channel and to provide long-range artillery support to the army and the navy as they launched the largest amphibious assault ever planned.

On the other side of the Channel, the British prepared to repel the expected invasion. Defences were constructed at possible landing sites to stop the German panzers and supporting infantry. Old rail guns were moved to the coast and the first long-range batteries were installed. These were employed to interdict enemy shipping and destroy, or at least deplete, any invasion force before it even landed. Generals Alan Brooke (Commander-in-Chief Home Forces) and Hastings Ismay (Churchill's chief staff officer and military adviser) were not convinced of their value, and their scepticism was understandable. 'Winnie' and 'Pooh', two old naval guns installed near Dover, had no fire control and as such could not hit enemy shipping; and 'Boche Buster' – an 18in. rail gun – did not have the range to reach the French coast. The shortcomings of these big guns were laid bare in 1942 when the British failed to stop the Channel Dash by the German capital ships *Gneisenau*, *Prinz Eugen* and *Scharnhorst*. This caused anger and embarrassment in Britain, and in private Churchill was quick to blame radar – but this new technology was soon to show its worth. British heavy coastal guns, using radar to track enemy vessels and watch the fall of shot, were able to engage German ships with impressive results.

One of the massive 40.6cm guns of Batterie 'Lindemann' being moved into place. The gun is sitting on a Gotha multi-axle trailer. In the background is one of the enormous gantries that were used to lift the gun from the trailer and position it in the gun cradle. The photo was used for propaganda purposes, where in December 1942 it was described thus: 'Travelling giant! War march of a giant gun to the Atlantic.' (akg-images/Sammlung Berliner Verlag/Archiv, AKG5568487)

Later in the war, with the fighting strength of the Luftwaffe much diminished, the Allies utilized aerial observation to direct fire. This was critical in September 1944 when the coastal batteries around Dover supported the Canadian infantry attack on the German cross-Channel guns. Unlike the British guns that were lightly protected in open positions, many of the German heavy coastal guns were emplaced in reinforced concrete casemates. These were impervious to all but the heaviest Allied bombs, but did limit the guns' traverse. Most could only fire out to sea, and as such the Canadians, who had been given the less than glamourous job of clearing the Channel ports, were largely untroubled by the German heavy guns as they advanced. Instead, the German crews targeted the coastal towns of Kent, which suffered the most devastating shelling of the war.

Whilst the massive German guns had not troubled the Canadians as they rolled up the Atlantic Wall and captured the deep-water ports, the cross-Channel batteries did give Allied planners food for thought when they were formulating ideas for invading 'Fortress Europe'. The 'hard snout' around Calais, although the shortest and most direct route to Berlin, was not genuinely considered as a landing site, because the fortifications there were so strong. Instead, they chose Normandy, which was less well defended and therefore offered a greater chance of success. The downside was that the landing beaches were further from Germany and gave the defenders valuable time to continue and indeed intensify their bombardment of southern England. Launch sites were constructed in France for V-1 missiles, which could reach London, and work started on a 'supergun' (see Osprey Fortress 72: *German V-Weapon Sites 1943–45*).

A famous propaganda photograph of a German K12 N rail gun firing across the English Channel in 1941. Inspired by the World War I 'Paris Gun', the two 21cm K12s could comfortably hit the coastal towns of Kent from their bases in France. (SeM/Universal Images Group via Getty Images)

Fortunately, this weapon was never used; heavy bombing and then Canadian land forces moving up from the south ensured that it was never completed.

Residents of south-east England would be grateful for this small mercy. Since the start of the war, they had been bombed and strafed by the Luftwaffe, had been targeted with V-1 rockets and had borne the brunt of the cross-Channel shelling. Initially, the towns of south-east England were seen as easy targets for the German gunners, but increasingly they were targeted in retaliation for British shelling. The people living near the guns complained, especially when shells were fired at night or in poor weather when there was seemingly no chance of hitting anything. They were unaware that radar made firing blind feasible, and believed the gunners were simply 'letting off steam'. Though frustrating for local residents, the British shelling provided a small but valuable opportunity to get back at the Germans. This was vital for morale in a country where in the first part of the war all the news had been bad: the British Expeditionary Force (BEF) had been defeated; at sea HMS *Hood* had been sunk and U-boats were menacing merchant ships in the Atlantic; and in the skies the Luftwaffe was seemingly able to bomb British towns and cities at will.

Significantly, the cross-Channel guns were also a powerful propaganda tool. At the start of the war, many dignitaries visited the big British guns and cameras captured them firing – footage that was played in cinemas up and down the country.

Across the Channel, the heavy German guns were also a potent propaganda weapon. Newsreels and *Signal* magazine showed the massive guns bombarding Britain, which, along with the Luftwaffe and the U-boats, would soon bring Britain to its knees. Later, they would be used to convince a war-weary nation that the Atlantic Wall was impregnable. This did have a kernel of truth. The RAF carried out a number of bombing raids against the reinforced concrete shelters that protected the rail and coastal guns, but could not silence them. And nor could the British coastal guns, which in September 1944 shelled their counterparts until their barrels were worn out. Some damage was caused, but it was not until the end of September when Canadian ground forces attacked that the German guns were silenced – the old military adage still held, 'artillery conquers and infantry occupies'.

The coastal towns of Kent now enjoyed peace for the first time in four years and work started to repair the damage. At the same time, the British military took the opportunity to review the peacetime requirement for coastal defence. The large rail guns were scrapped and 'Winnie' and 'Pooh' were removed. A little over a decade later, all the large-calibre guns had gone, and today little remains. In France the guns were removed, but many of the reinforced concrete bunkers have survived – the only tangible reminder of an oft-forgotten duel.

CHRONOLOGY

1939
3 September   France and Great Britain declare war on Germany.

1940
10 May   Germany launches the offensive in West.
26 May   Dunkirk evacuation starts.
22 June   France signs armistice with Germany.
Summer   Work begins on cross-Channel guns 'Oldenburg', 'Prinz Heinrich', 'Grosser Kurfürst', 'Friedrich August' and 'Todt'.
August   Kent shelled for first time. 'Winnie' responds.
December   Hitler visits Cap Gris-Nez.

1941
February   'Boche Buster' deployed to Kent.
22 June   Germany invades USSR.

1942
January   South Foreland completed.
February   Fritz Todt, Reich Minister for Armaments and Munitions, is killed in an air crash.
February   The Channel Dash takes place. New Batterie 'Todt' inaugurated.
March   'Jane' is completed.
May   'Clem' is completed.
August   British raid on Dieppe.

1943
March   'Bruce' is test-fired.
July   'Winnie' and 'Pooh' are put into care and maintenance.
October   Work starts on V-3 'supergun'.

1944
20 January   MV *Walkenried* is sunk by the British.
May   'Winnie' and 'Pooh' are restored to action.
6 June   Operation *Overlord*: Allies land in Normandy. SS *Sambut* is sunk by the Germans.
25 August   Paris is liberated.
Early/mid-September   German batteries are shelled from the UK.
End September   Canadians capture the German guns and the shelling stops.

1945
7 May   German unconditional surrender is signed.

Rail guns

Name	Location/date entered service	Range (max.)
1. Boche Buster	Bishopsbourne (February 1941)	20.391km
2. Gladiator	Guston (May 1941)	44.7km
3. Piecemaker	Guston (November 1940)	44.7km
4. Scene Shifter	Guston (September 1940)	44.7km
5. Cleo	Shepherdswell (September 1940)	13.122km
6. Sheba	Shepherdswell (September 1940)	13.122km

Fixed cross-Channel batteries

Battery	Location	Range (max.)
7. Winnie	St Margaret's at Cliffe	46.63km
8. Pooh	St Margaret's at Cliffe	46.63km
9. Jane	Wanstone	38.405km
10. Clem	Wanstone	38.405km
11. Bruce*	St Margaret's at Cliffe	100.548km
12. South Foreland	South Foreland	33.56km

* Note: there is no evidence that Bruce fired across the Channel.

Other

Name	Location
13. Dummy Winnie	S: Margaret's at Cliffe
14. Dummy Pooh	S: Margaret's at Cliffe

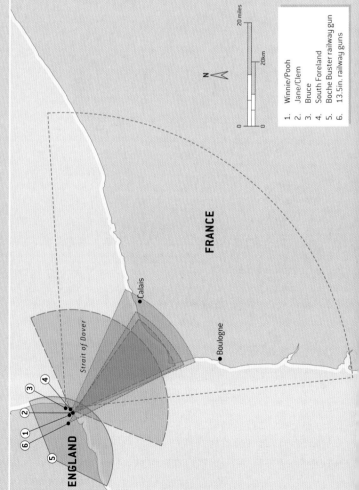

N

ENGLAND

Strait of Dover

Calais

Boulogne

FRANCE

1. Winnie/Pooh
2. Jane/Clem
3. Bruce
4. South Foreland
5. Boche Buster railway gun
6. 13.5in. railway guns

0   20km
0   20 miles

Guston

Dover

Dover Castle

St Margaret's at Cliffe

N

0   2km
0   2 miles

DESIGN AND DEVELOPMENT

BRITISH

STATIC GUNS

As an island nation, Britain had a long tradition of defending its coast against potential invaders. In the 16th century, Henry VIII built a series of fortifications on the coast to mount artillery that could be used against enemy ships. Fast forward to the 19th century, Martello towers were constructed to counter any threat from Napoleon. In the second half of the century, Palmerston Forts were erected to deter a resurgent France. In World War I, some of these Victorian coastal forts were modernized to combat the menace from the Germans who were now ensconced just across the Channel. In addition, trenches and gun positions were dug and the first concrete pillboxes in England were located at likely invasion points. However, little thought had been given to the possibility of a German naval bombardment of the coast, because for so long the Royal Navy had ruled the waves. This oversight was cruelly exposed when Hartlepool, Scarborough and Whitby were attacked in December 1914. The immediate response was the installation of new coastal artillery batteries. These provided some protection to the mainland but did not prevent a further attack in April 1916 when Yarmouth and Lowestoft were bombarded. Following the Battle of Jutland in June 1916, the German fleet was effectively confined to port and the British mainland was not threatened again.

After the war, many of these coastal gun positions were retained. They were expensive to install, and if they were effective and serviceable, it made sense to keep

OPPOSITE
British cross-Channel batteries.

The Battery Observation Post (BOP) for both guns at Wanstone – 'Jane' and 'Clem' – taken in April 1942. This position enabled spotters to identify targets and relay details to the guns. Spoil has been used on the top and at the sides of the position to provide added protection and for camouflage. (Dover Museum)

them. Some new guns were installed in the interwar period, but funds were limited; with no immediate threat to the British Isles, money was allocated to other defence priorities, including the protection of overseas territories. However, Britain's ability to safeguard her interests in the Far East was limited under the terms of the Washington Naval Treaty of 1922. This was signed by Britain, France, Italy, Japan and the US and placed restrictions not only on capital ships but also naval bases. Significantly, Singapore was unaffected by the terms of the treaty. Plans to fortify the new naval base had been proposed in the 1920s, though it was another decade before work began. Initially, works were small-scale (6in. and 9.2in. guns), but later, in response to the growing threat from Japan, five large BL 15in. Mk I naval guns were installed. Three guns were located in Changi and formed the Johore Battery, which defended the route to the large naval base located at Sembawang. Two further 15in. guns were located at Buona Vista.

The guns were completed by the start of the war and Singapore was now well protected against any attack from the Imperial Japanese Navy. The same could not be said for the British Isles. Two decades after the Treaty of Versailles, Britain was again at war with Germany. A review of coastal defences in September 1939 found Dover's defences to be outdated and inadequate. To make matters worse, coastal defence had been given over to the Territorial Army – well-trained but part-time gunners. The Phoney War allowed some improvements to port defences and this work was accelerated in 1940 after Germany's attack in the West. 'Emergency batteries' were installed which consisted of smaller-calibre guns that could be used to provide direct fire on an enemy trying to invade. (The tunnels under Dover Castle were also extended and included a Coastal Artillery HQ.)

Later, at the behest of Churchill, long-range coastal guns were installed. An unintended, but now welcome, consequence of the Washington Naval Treaty was that Britain had established a significant stockpile of naval guns. These guns were much bigger (8in. to 15in.) and had a greater range. They were now quickly moved to the

coast and employed in specially prepared positions for coastal defence. Significantly, the guns were provided with observation posts, range-finding equipment, plotting rooms and later radar.

The need to change the gun barrels on a regular basis meant that the coastal guns could not be protected by concrete bunkers. As such, camouflage was immensely important. The scrim to hide the guns was manufactured from fire-retardant materials to avoid catching fire, and the camouflage for 'Winnie' and 'Pooh' was reputedly designed by the stage magician Jasper Maskelyne. Dummy sites for 'Winnie' and 'Pooh' were also constructed to confuse and distract the Germans.

RAIL

The British Army was by tradition small and professional and had no great need of heavy artillery and certainly not rail guns. This changed in World War I when the fighting descended into a bloody stalemate. The British now became obsessed with heavy artillery and, following the German and French example, developed their own rail guns. Initially, the rail guns were modest in size with 9.2in. and 12in. versions developed. These guns could bring significant fire to bear before being redeployed without having to rely on a muddy and often clogged road system. After the armistice, as the British demobilized, these guns were dismantled and mothballed. This withdrawal from service proved only temporary, and at the outbreak of World War II, these guns were dusted off and were moved to the coast to cover possible landing sites, or as a mobile reserve. Some 12in. railway guns were sent to France in 1939, but they were abandoned in the haphazard retreat and were captured by the Germans in 1940.

The genesis of the large-calibre rail guns deployed to Kent in 1940 can also be traced to World War I. In 1916, it had been decided to mount two 14in. guns, originally destined for the Japanese navy, on railway carriages. The guns arrived on the Western Front in May 1918 and were in action in the summer. The two guns were known as HM Gun 'Boche Buster' and HM Gun 'Scene Shifter'. (King George V personally oversaw the firing of the first shell by HMG 'Boche Buster' on 8 August 1918 and became known as 'The King's Shot'.) Though they fired more than 200

rounds during the final four months of the war, the 14in. gun was not a standard British service calibre, and the guns were declared obsolete in 1926 and scrapped. The two carriages, along with two others that had been ordered, were put into storage. In 1940, following the fall of France, three of these rail carriages were recovered from store and refurbished and adapted to mount a 13.5in. gun. These gun barrels had been designed before World War I to be fitted to British dreadnoughts including the Iron Duke class. After the London Naval Treaty of 1930, the Iron Duke class was decommissioned and their gun barrels placed in reserve. The three rail guns were ready by May 1941 and used the names originally given to the carriages in World War I – 'Scene Shifter', 'Gladiator' and 'Piecemaker'.

The route of HMG 'Boche Buster' to Bishopsbourne in Kent in February 1941 was slightly different. As has been mentioned, a rail gun with this name was deployed on the Western Front in World War I, but at this time mounted a 14in. gun. The British High Command on the Western Front, confronted with the challenge of breaching the concrete pillboxes and barbed wire of the German Hindenburg Line, requested an 18in. gun that could be mounted on the same rail carriage. However, there were no existing barrels of that calibre and a new one had to be produced. The Elswick Ordnance Company in Newcastle and Vickers were contracted to make the barrels, but they were not completed until after the end of the war. The barrel was tested, but the barrels and the rail carriage to mount them were put into store. At the start of World War II, Major (later Lieutenant-Colonel) S.M. Cleeve, RA who had served with 'Boche Buster' in World War I, scoured the naval and army stores and recovered the 18in. barrels. In October 1940, one of the barrels was married with the 'Boche Buster' rail mounting. The gun and its crew were put through their paces at Catterick before the behemoth was shunted south and deployed on the Elham Valley Railway.

One of the Chain Home Low radar stations. These were installed along the south coast of England and were used by the British coastal gun batteries to target enemy shipping. They were pivotal in denying the Germans free passage through the Channel and helped the gunners to sink 28 ships. (Dover Museum)

RADAR

At the start of the war, fire direction for coastal artillery had not evolved markedly from the techniques used in the 19th century. A series of Observation Posts (OPs) would communicate the range and bearing of the target to the Fortress Plotting Room (FPR). The staff here translated this information into coordinates for the guns, which were adjusted as the fall of shot was observed.

However, direct observation of targets was not possible at night or in bad weather, and here radar – a detection system that uses radio waves – had a huge impact on fire control. Early work in this area had established that it was possible to develop a radar that was capable of detecting ships. In April 1938, the General Staff gave conditional approval for work on a coast defence radar. This evolved into two distinct work streams:

(1) Coast Defence (CD) radar, which was principally concerned with detection of enemy craft.

(2) Coast Artillery (CA) radar, which was to provide fire direction for coastal artillery (though early radars were often used for both purposes).

In July 1939, work commenced on a CD radar that was capable of detecting ships and low-flying aircraft. The RAF version was given the codename Chain Home Low (CHL) and for the Army CD/CHL. Two sets were installed – one at Lydden Spout and one at Fan Hole – which gave the battery early warning of enemy movements. In a live-fire exercise in July 1939, radar detected shell splashes from a 9.2in. gun when it missed its target. This meant that the gunners could then correct their fire onto the target in the same way that they would if provided the range and bearing by an observer.

Coincident with this work, the Admiralty developed the Naval Type 271 radar. In July 1941, this radar was trialled in Dover and allowed Vice Admiral Sir Bertram Ramsay (Commander-in-Chief, Dover) to see craft in the Channel – even small, fast-moving E-boats. This radar was kept at Dover and further sets – known as the CD No. 1 Mk 4 – were also installed. In November 1941, and later in February 1942, an attempt was made to fire on E-boats in the Channel using radar, but the boats altered

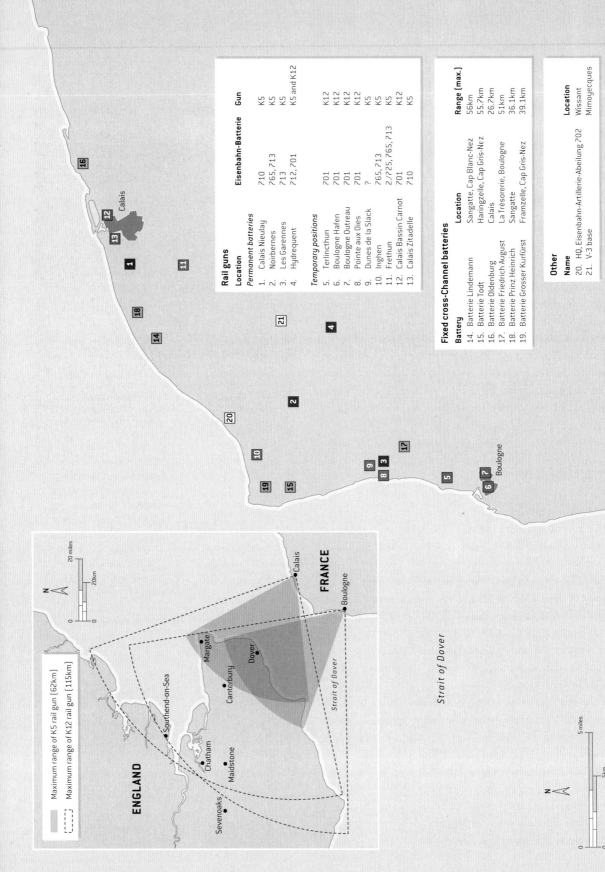

Rail guns

Location	Eisenbahn-Batterie	Gun
Permanent batteries		
1. Calais Nieulay	710	K5
2. Noirbernes	765, 713	K5
3. Les Garennes	713	K5
4. Hydrequent	712, 701	K5 and K12
Temporary positions		
5. Terlincthun	701	K12
6. Boulogne Hafen	701	K12
7. Boulogne Outreau	701	K12
8. Pointe aux Oies	701	K12
9. Dunes de la Slack	?	K5
10. Inghen	765, 713	K5
11. Frethun	2,725, 765, 713	K5
12. Calais Bassin Carnot	701	K12
13. Calais Zitadelle	710	K5

Fixed cross-Channel batteries

Battery	Location	Range (max.)
14. Batterie Lindemann	Sangatte, Cap Blanc-Nez	56km
15. Batterie Todt	Haringzelle, Cap Gris-Nez	55.7km
16. Batterie Oldenburg	Calais	26.7km
17. Batterie Friedrich August	La Trésorerie, Boulogne	51km
18. Batterie Prinz Heinrich	Sangatte	36.1km
19. Batterie Grosser Kurfürst	Framzelle, Cap Gris-Nez	39.1km

Other

Name	Location
20. HQ, Eisenbahn-Artillerie-Abeilung 702	Wissant
21. V-3 base	Mimoyecques

Maximum range of K5 rail gun (62km)
Maximum range of K12 rail gun (115km)

ENGLAND
FRANCE
Sevenoaks
Maidstone
Chatham
Southend-on-Sea
Canterbury
Margate
Dover
Calais
Boulogne
Strait of Dover

course out of range of the guns. Although unsuccessful, the concept had been proven. The next test for the CD radar came in the same month when the Germans moved three of their major warships through the Channel. British coastal artillery engaged the enemy, but could not stop them. Churchill was clear that the poor showing was down to the shortcomings of radar, and in part he was right. Without the operators noticing, the Germans had been able to jam the radars covering the coast, so reducing their effectiveness. However, this general criticism was rebutted by the radar pioneer Robert Watson-Watt – and development continued.

Drawing on advances made by the three services, CD/CHL sets were adapted for coastal artillery use. This led to the development of the CA No. 1 Mk 1 and 2 sets (which used parts from the Royal Navy's NT271 radar). These were installed at Wanstone from the summer of 1942 and their impact was immediate, with significant improvements in the accuracy of fire as operators observed enemy movements and the brief but obvious return of shell splashes on the radar sets and adjusted their fire accordingly.

Batterie 'Pommern' consisted of a single naval gun installed by the Germans on the Belgium coast in World War I. The 38cm SK L/45 gun was protected by an armoured cab and was unique in that it engaged land-based Allied targets around Dunkirk and Ypres. After the Armistice of November 1918, the gun was a popular tourist destination. (Author's collection)

GERMAN

STATIC GUNS

The idea of installing old naval guns in fixed positions was used extensively by the Germans in World War I and was copied and expanded in World War II. As early as October 1914, the Army ordered six carriages that could take either a 38cm or 35.5cm gun. The first of these, mounting a 35.5cm gun, was installed in Belgium and was ready in April 1915. A further five carriages were completed along the Western Front by the end of the year. However, the concrete base took six weeks to complete and limited the gun's mobility, so the concept was abandoned. In the winter of 1917/18, to support the Spring Offensive, the Germans revived the idea and constructed a number of *Betonbettungen* (concrete foundations) to mount 38cm SK L/45 'Langer Max' or Long Max guns. At the same time, a simple carriage was designed and built by Krupp that reduced the time it took to position the gun and provided greater mobility. The *Eisenbahn und Bettungsgeschütz* (railway and platform mounted gun) allowed guns to be fired from a suitable section of track or from a pre-prepared position. From May 1918, this design was exclusively used.

The Germans also adopted the idea of using large naval guns for coastal defence in Belgium. Building on their experience along the Baltic and North Sea coast, the navy constructed ten heavy coastal batteries that covered the whole of the Belgian coast.

These defences were particularly strong near the front line, but also around the main ports of Ostend and Zeebrugge.

OPPOSITE
The German cross-Channel batteries.

Table 1: German static battery locations			
Batterie	Location	No.	Calibre
Braunschweig	Zoute	4	28cm SK L/40
Deutschland	Bredene	4	38cm SK L/45
Hannover	De Haan	3	28cm SK L/40
Hessen	Zeebrugge	3	28cm SK L/40
Hindenburg	Ostend	4	28cm K L/35
Groden*	Blankenberge	4	28cm Hb L/12 Howitzer
Kaiser Wilhelm II	Knokke	4	30.5cm SK L/50
Pommern	Koekelare	1	38cm SK L/45
Preussen	Bredene	4	28cm SK L/40
Tirpitz	Ostend	4	28cm SK L/45

* Unlike the other heavy batteries, 'Groden' mounted howitzers that only covered the sea front.

In October 1914, the Navy established Batterie 'Tirpitz' south-west of Ostend with four 28cm guns in *Geschützbrunnen* (circular concrete gun pits). Also in Ostend, near Fort Napoleon, four old 28cm K L/35 guns in armoured turrets were set in semi-circular concrete positions. These guns had been moved from Wilhelmshaven in 1915 and were christened Batterie 'Hindenburg'. In September 1915, the Navy ordered four more carriages to mount surplus 30.5cm SK L/50 guns. These positions were completed in April 1916 and became known as Batterie 'Kaiser Wilhelm II'.

In June 1916, the Navy decided to position two 38cm gun batteries to protect the U-boat pens constructed on the Belgium coast. These guns were to be installed on a *Bettungsschiessgerüst* (platform firing framework). Four guns that had originally been destined for the Western Front were installed at Bredene and were christened Batterie 'Deutschland'. Another gun was installed at Koekelare and was called Batterie 'Pommern'. This gun was unique in that, although located on the coast, it was only able to fire in a restricted arc inland.

The *Eisenbahn und Bettungsgeschütz* was also used on the Flanders coast with concrete foundations poured to mount the rail turntables (the gun was moved into place, the rail removed and the gun secured with bolts). These were used for the 28cm SK L/40 'Brunos' installed at batteries 'Braunschweig', 'Hannover', 'Hessen' and 'Preussen'.

As the tide of the war turned and the Allies advanced, the German Navy destroyed the Belgium coastal guns. After the war, under the terms of the Treaty of Versailles, Germany was not allowed to extend or improve its fortifications. However, because the bulk of the coast defences on the Baltic and North Sea were considered defensive in nature, they were not significantly impacted by the settlement. Heligoland was demilitarized, but the six guns on Wangerooge remained. After the Nazi's accession power, Hitler ordered that two of these guns – 30.5cm SK L/50 guns from Batterie 'Friedrich August' – should be moved to the southern sector of the West Wall, where they became Batterie 'Ottenhöfen'. These guns were later moved to La Trésorerie just north of Boulogne, where their original name was restored. Similarly, the 24cm

SK L/50 guns originally installed on Borkum Island in the North Sea were moved to a prepared position in the southern Black Forest at the start of World War II, and were later moved to Calais and became Batterie 'Oldenburg'.

RAIL

In World War I, the Germans also mounted surplus naval guns on rail carriages. The Navy had cancelled the construction of a number of capital ships in favour of U-boat production, which meant that additional guns were available to use. Other barrels were freed up after the Battle of Jutland in June 1916 when ships deemed obsolete were withdrawn from service.

The most famous of these rail guns was the Paris Gun (Paris-Geschütz) which was developed by Krupp. Seven old 38cm SK L/45 gun barrels were used, which were fitted with an internal tube that reduced the calibre to 21cm. The total barrel length was 37m and was capable of firing a shell 130km (81 miles). The gun was mounted on a special rail carriage and fired from a concrete emplacement with a turntable. It was first used in March 1918, and over the next six months fired more than 300 shells. In August 1918, the gun was withdrawn to Germany to avoid capture by the advancing Allies.

After the war, the Allies banned Germany from developing long-range guns under the terms of the peace agreed at Versailles. However, Krupp continued theoretical work. After the Nazis came to power in 1933, they funded the research and Krupp was able to translate its plans into a refined Paris Gun, which became the 21cm K12 (E). In 1934, Krupp also began work on a 28cm railway gun – the K5 – and in 1936, an initial test-firing took place. A few years later, the rail guns were used in anger.

During the war, ammunition for the K5 and K12 rail guns was adapted and improved. This allowed the guns to fire much further. The compromise was that the payload was smaller. Alternative methods for delivering a larger payload led to the development of the V-1 flying bomb (a missile that used a pulse-jet engine for power) and the V-2, the first long-range guided ballistic missile. However, the idea of a long-range gun was not dead.

V-3

The apotheosis of the cross-Channel guns was the Vergeltungswaffe 3 (Vengeance Weapon), or V-3. Although a vengeance weapon, the V-3 was not a rocket but a 'supergun' – a large-calibre gun using multiple-charges to add velocity to a projectile (the V-3 was also known as the Hochdruckpumpe or High-Pressure Pump – a codename designed to disguise the true aim of the project). The guns were to be installed in France on two adjacent sites – east and west – approximately 1km apart. Each site was to have five inclined shafts fitted with five V-3 'superguns'. The 50 guns were to be aimed at London, some 165km away, and when operational each site could notionally fire 600 rounds every hour.

Early in 1943, engineers identified a suitable site at Mimoyecques in northern France. The limestone hill was ideal for the inclined tunnels that would house the gun tubes and the galleries to house support equipment and for the movement and storage of ammunition. Construction work on the rail lines started in September 1943, and

The V-3 'supergun' site at Mimoyecques was targeted by Allied bombers, most famously by the Dambusters, which dropped 'Tallboy' bombs on the site. At least one of these smashed through the reinforced concrete roof. Some of the damage is still visible today. (Author's photograph)

a month later the Organisation Todt, utilizing slave labour, started excavation work. The scale of this work was staggering. The shafts for the guns were 105m long, with the vertical elevator shafts that served the guns descending to a depth of 80m. On the surface, a huge concrete slab 5.5m thick protected the facility. This was perforated with five openings, which were protected with steel plates when the weapon was not in use.

Fearing that the site was a possible V-2 launch site, the Allies bombed the complex on a number of occasions, which seriously disrupted the work and forced the abandonment of the western site. In spite of the setbacks, the Germans planned to have the first five guns ready to fire in March 1944, and the site fully operational by October.

On 6 July 1944, 617 Squadron – the Dambusters – targeted the complex with 'Tallboy' bombs. Initially, it was unclear what impact the raid had had, but subsequent investigation showed that one of the so-called 'earthquake bombs' had hit one of the shafts and exploded underground. Debris blocked underground galleries, but also tragically killed a number of slave workers. Work at Mimoyecques was finally halted in September 1944 when Canadian forces overran the site. The complex was destroyed by the British after the war.

RADAR

In Germany, the development of radar was being progressed by a number of companies. The Gesellschaft für Electroakustische und Mechanische Apparate (GEMA) was established in 1934. Its work was presented to Grossadmiral Erich Raeder, CinC of the Kriegsmarine, who could see the potential of the technology and agreed to fund further work, which led to the development of the Seetakt and Freya series of radars.

However, the Kriegsmarine was conservative in its approach to radar. It envisaged Seetakt as a tool for ranging and not for the detection of vessels at night or in poor visibility and certainly not fire control. The Kriegsmarine also kept its work on radar under wraps – Hermann Göring, the Commander-in-Chief of the Luftwaffe, did not find out about the navy's work on radar until July 1938, and was outraged.

Early versions of the radars were installed before the war on Heligoland, Borkum and Sylt where large German coastal batteries were located. The Freya radar was used to detect ships and the Seetakt for fire direction. When these guns were moved to the coast of France in the summer of 1940, so were the radars. Soon they were in action. In November 1940, under the cover of darkness, a British convoy moved through the Channel and was shelled. This worried the British, who established that a Seetakt radar was being used to direct fire. To reduce its effectiveness, it was jammed from March 1941.

In parallel with the work of GEMA, Telefunken was also developing radars. In 1939, it produced the Würzburg or FuMG 62A – later renamed FuMG 39(T). It was unique in a number of ways, not least the steerable paraboloid dish antenna (the Freya and Seetakt radars – and British CHL – were vertical arrays). Four different variants were developed during the war (A to D) each improving on the previous one. (A Würzburg A was captured by the British in the Bruneval raid of February 1942.) In the war, the radars were used in concert – the Freya would detect the target and the details were sent to the more accurate Würzburg, which would track the enemy and pass details to the gunners.

However, it was recognized that even the Würzburg D lacked the range and accuracy needed, so Zeppelin (the airship manufacturer) was contracted to develop a new, larger dish. This became known as the Würzburg Riese or Giant Würzburg (FuMO 214) and was used by the Kriegsmarine to watch the coast and for directing fire. This radar was used at Cran aux Oeufs to guide the firing of Batterie 'Todt'.

THE STRATEGIC SITUATION

THE OPPOSING FORCES

When considering the strengths of the opposing forces, it is important to look at the wider picture and not simply examine the cross-Channel guns in isolation. As a maritime nation, Britain looked to its senior service – the Royal Navy – to command the English Channel. However, Britain was a world power and although the Royal Navy was significantly bigger than the Kriegsmarine, the Royal Navy also had to police the key trade routes. In doing this, it was challenged by the Germans in the Atlantic, the Italians in the Mediterranean and the Japanese in the Far East. In spite of this, the Navy did carry out a number of operations in the Channel, but the size and frequency was limited, because the Admiralty was worried about the German coastal batteries and potential air attacks.

In the skies above the Channel in the summer of 1940, the Luftwaffe was pre-eminent. After the defeat of France, Göring's air force attacked convoys and coastal targets in the so-called *Kanalkampf*, and for a short period of time the British were unable to use the Channel. In August, the Luftwaffe was ordered to target the RAF in an attempt to secure air superiority, and it almost succeeded; but by October 1940, the Battle of Britain was over – the RAF had prevailed.

At sea, the Kriegsmarine enjoyed some significant successes – notably the sinking of the *Hood* in 1941 – but the Royal Navy now sought revenge and hunted the

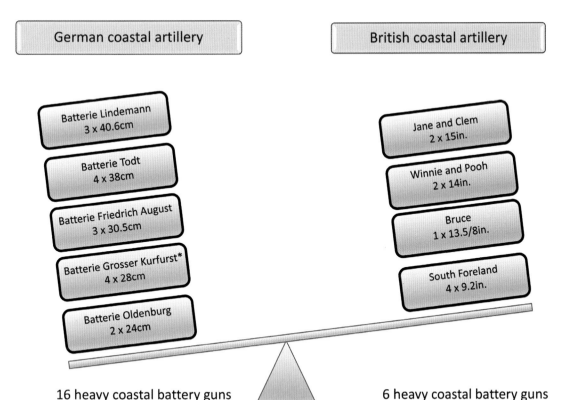

German coastal artillery	British coastal artillery

Batterie Lindemann
3 x 40.6cm

Batterie Todt
4 x 38cm

Batterie Friedrich August
3 x 30.5cm

Batterie Grosser Kurfurst*
4 x 28cm

Batterie Oldenburg
2 x 24cm

Jane and Clem
2 x 15in.

Winnie and Pooh
2 x 14in.

Bruce
1 x 13.5/8in.

South Foreland
4 x 9.2in.

16 heavy coastal battery guns

6 heavy coastal battery guns

* Replacing Prinz Heinrich 2 x 28cm

German surface fleet. Some, like the *Bismarck*, were chased down, engaged and sent to the bottom; other capital ships were forced to seek sanctuary in safe harbours.

Unlike their compatriots at sea, the German naval gunners manning the batteries around Calais always held the upper hand, both in terms of protection, but also the number of guns and the calibre of weapons. This can clearly be seen in the graphic 'Coastal artillery: German vs British'.

In addition, German K5 and K12 rail guns were moved to the French coast in preparation for Operation *Sea Lion*. In 1941, some of these guns were moved east to support the invasion of the Soviet Union, but they soon returned to France to bombard Britain again. In 1943, there was a plan to move the massive rail guns 'Dora' and 'Gustav' to Calais, but this was shelved and instead the Germans concentrated on the deployment of V-1 and V-2 missiles.

On the other side of the Channel, the British were always playing catch-up. At the start of the war, they constructed emergency coastal batteries to protect ports and harbours. These were mostly old naval guns of smaller calibre – 4in. to 6in. Later, larger-calibre coastal guns were installed at Fan Bay (3 x 6in.), Lydden Spout (3 x 6in.), Capel, (3 x 8in.) and Hougham (3 x 8in.). However, there were only ever three genuine long-range batteries (Bruce never fired in anger) – South Foreland, the 14in. guns at St Margaret's at Cliffe and Wanstone. Numerically they were inferior to their foe, and they

Coastal artillery: German vs British.

An image showing 'Pooh' with the 14in. gun installed on its cradle. The armoured cab is now being added to protect the crew. Unlike the German guns, it was not possible to add a concrete roof and surround, because of the need to change the barrel. The whole position has been heavily camouflaged. (Dover Museum)

also suffered by being installed in open emplacements with only armoured cabs to protect the crew rather than reinforced concrete. The coastal batteries were supplemented by rail guns, but they were typically outnumbered 2:1, and only the three 13.5in. rail guns had the range to hit France; 'Boche Buster', an 18in. howitzer, could only fire halfway across the Channel.

In the final reckoning, the German dominance was not critical because the Allies were pre-eminent at sea and in the air. After D-Day, the Allies used their naval power to pound German coastal positions, including the long-range guns around Calais. In the air, the Allies enjoyed near-total superiority. Bombing raids against strategic targets grew in size and frequency and included attacks on German coastal batteries. However, the reinforced concrete casemates were impervious to the attacks, and the guns continued to operate until eventually overrun by ground forces.

STRATEGY

BRITISH

In the period after Britain's declaration of war on Germany – the so-called 'Phoney War' – the British were not idle. General Sir Walter Kirke, CinC Home Forces, was ordered to prepare a plan for repelling a German attack on the British Isles. In November 1939, he presented his 'Julius Caesar' Plan, which outlined how the limited home forces would be deployed to protect the eastern coast of England and Scotland, especially airfields and ports. At that time, the General Staff was confident that the plan would not be needed. The massive forts of the Maginot Line protected France's border with Germany, and the powerful French Army, supplemented by the BEF, was, on paper, more than capable of defeating the Wehrmacht should it strike through the Benelux countries.

This confidence was dented in April 1940 following the German invasion of Denmark and Norway, and shattered after the attack on the Low Countries and France in May 1940. The German blitzkrieg, or lightning warfare, soon overwhelmed the British and French forces, and at the end of May what remained of the BEF was evacuated from Dunkirk. This prompted feverish activity in Britain to improve home defences. On 27 May 1940, General Sir Edmund Ironside replaced Kirke as CinC Home Forces. On the same day, the Home Defence Executive, chaired by Ironside, was established. Its primary concern was organizing the defence of Britain. The Executive ordered the creation of a series of 'stop lines' made up of pillboxes and anti-tank defences constructed to slow or stop any invasion force. Importantly, it also ordered the construction of coastal defences, especially in southern and eastern England, in what became known as the 'coastal crust'. Possible landing sites were protected with anti-tank defences, barbed wire and mines. Pillboxes were constructed to the rear to provide an element of protection for the defenders and bring deadly fire to bear on any attacker. Significantly, emergency coastal batteries were also constructed to protect ports and harbours. Later, bigger coastal batteries were constructed to mount guns, up to 15in., to deny the Channel to enemy shipping, destroy or diminish an invasion force and counter enemy guns on the Continent.

GERMAN

German strategy, as had been the case in World War I, was determined by the need to avoid a war on two fronts. Therefore, although the Wehrmacht had enjoyed startling success in defeating Denmark and Norway, seizing the Low Countries and France, and expelling the BEF from the Continent, it was essential that Britain either sued for peace or was defeated. To achieve this, German U-boats would target merchant vessels and the Luftwaffe would defeat the RAF and secure air superiority – Göring promised that this would be achieved by the end of August 1940. If Britain continued to resist, an invasion was planned – Operation *Seelöwe*. In an OKW directive on 10 July 1940, Generaloberst Wilhelm Keitel detailed artillery protection for the planned invasion: 'All preparations will be made for strong artillery support on the coast line from Calais (Cap Gris-Nez) to Boulogne to cover a future crossing and landing. Under command CinC Navy, all available and suitable heavy batteries will be installed in fixed positions by the Todt Organization.'

On 16 July 1940, Hitler issued Führer Directive No. 16 formalizing preparations for a landing in Britain. One of the four preconditions for the invasion set out in Hitler's directive was that the coastal zone between occupied France and England must be dominated by heavy coastal artillery to close the Strait of Dover to Royal Navy warships and merchant convoys. Work to emplace heavy artillery along the French coast, especially around the Pas-de-Calais, started on 22 July 1940.

Interestingly, in that same month, Hitler ordered preparations for an invasion of the Soviet Union, and in October 1940, with the RAF still undefeated, Operation *Sea Lion* was postponed. On 18 December 1940, Hitler issued Führer Directive No. 21 – Operation *Barbarossa*. This noted that the Wehrmacht would invade the Soviet Union even before the conclusion of the war against Britain. In June 1941, Hitler launched Operation *Barbarossa*, and in September Operation *Sea Lion* was cancelled.

As the threat of invasion diminished, the British launched small-scale actions in occupied Europe. Following the raid on the German radar station at Bruneval in February 1942, Hitler issued Führer Directive No. 40, which called for the creation of an 'Atlantic Wall' – a line of defences along the coast of continental Europe and Scandinavia. Particular attention was paid to the defence of ports and harbours following the raid on St Nazaire in the following month. The German cross-Channel guns dovetailed neatly into this plan. In November 1943, Hitler reinforced his commitment to this idea when he issued Führer Directive No. 51. In this, Hitler explained that he had, 'decided to strengthen the defences in the West, particularly at places from which we shall launch our long-range war against England'. This included the long-range guns around Calais and Boulogne.

TECHNICAL SPECIFICATIONS

BRITISH

RAIL GUNS

'Boche Buster' (18in.)

HMG 'Boche Buster' had originally been designed to mount a 14in. gun, but was later fitted with an 18in. gun with the same external measurements. This was feasible because, as a howitzer, the stresses on the barrel were less and as such the walls could be thinner. However, the lower barrel velocity also meant that it had a shorter range. The weapon could only fire circa 20km and could not reach France. With its limited traverse and slow rate of fire, it was not capable of engaging moving targets in the Channel. It was, though, a useful propaganda tool and was visited by a number of dignitaries, including the prime minister (PM), and was the subject of a Pathe newsreel in 1941.

The barrel and breech weighed 87 tonnes, which brought the all-in weight of the weapon to around 250 tonnes. The gun was mounted on a cradle that sat across two sets of bogies – eight axles fore and seven axles aft, making a total of 30 wheels. This spread the weight, but even so, steps had to be taken to strengthen the rail line.

'Boche Buster' fired a number of practice shells, but was not involved in any actual engagements. With the threat of invasion gone the gun was withdrawn from the coast and sent to Salisbury Plain, where it was involved in further firing trials using an anti-concrete shell. Some thought was given to the idea of deploying the gun in an invasion of continental Europe, but it was not progressed, and in 1947 the gun was scrapped.

'Piecemaker', 'Scene Shifter' and 'Gladiator' (13.5in.)

The gun mounting for 'Piecemaker', 'Scene Shifter' and 'Gladiator' was the same as 'Boche Buster'. The barrel was mounted in a cradle which sat atop two sets of bogies – eight at the front and seven at the back, which spread the 245-tonne mass. The rail carriages, originally designed to mount a 14in. gun, were adapted to take a 77-tonne 13.5in. Mk V gun. With a supercharge, these guns could fire a 567kg shell 44.7km – more than enough to reach France. However, to traverse they had to be shunted to suitable sections of curved track, which meant that they could not engage shipping in the Channel. Like 'Boche Buster', the three rail guns were

HMG 'Boche Buster' firing a shell in May 1941. The blast and recoil from the gun have raised a cloud of dust from the ballast on the train line. The curvature of the track allowed the gun to traverse and engage different targets. Despite the size of the gun and the impressive spectacle when firing, the rail gun did not have the range to reach France. (© Imperial War Museum, H9448)

withdrawn from the coast in 1943 and readied for a role supporting a cross-Channel invasion. However, in the end, air support was considered sufficient, and in 1945 they were scrapped.

'Sheba' and 'Cleo' (12in.)

A number of 12in. guns mounted on a rail platform had been used in World War I, but had been mothballed after the armistice. Just over 20 years later, they were restored and were again sent to France, but were lost in the disastrous retreat of 1940. More were available in the UK and 'Cleo' and 'Sheba', which had initially been stationed in Lincolnshire to cover the Humber Estuary, were moved to Kent after a visit by the PM. The guns were unique in that the barbette that mounted the gun sat in a well with two four-wheel bogies located at either end. This unique set-up allowed the gun to traverse 240 degrees using stabilizers to ensure the gun did not overbalance when fired. The 12in. gun could fire a 340kg shell a shade over 13km, so was only really useful for covering potential landing sites.

9.2in.

During World War I a number of 9.2in. guns were mounted on rail carriages, and after the war some of these were put into store. In 1940, they were hastily moved to Kent. The gun sat on a revolving platform that was fitted with a loading platform to allow the shells and charges to be moved to the breech. Four outriggers ensured that it remained stable when firing. The rail guns were armed with the Mk 10 (the same as the coast defence guns) and Mk 13 9.2in. guns, and had a maximum range of around 20km.

	'Boche Buster' 18In. (45.7cm)	'Piece Maker', 'Scene Shifter' and 'Gladiator' 13.5in. (34.3cm) Mk 5	'Sheba' and 'Cleo' 12in. (30.5cm) Mk 5	9.2in. (23.4cm) Mk 13
Table 2: British rail guns				
Weight (gun/ breech)	87,076kg (191,968lb)	77,347kg (170,520lb)	10,726kg (23,646lb)	24,614kg (54,264lb)
Total weight	254,438kg (560,935lb)	244,590kg (539,224lb)	77,176kg (170,143lb)	88,372kg (194,824lb)
Length of bore	15.865m (624.6in.) 35-cal.	15.431m (607.5in.) 45-cal.	5.273m (207.6in.) 17.3-cal.	8.179m (322in.) 35-cal.
Length	16.469m (648.4in.)	15.898m (625.9in.)	5.723m (225.3in.)	8.509m (335in.)
Rifling	72 grooves	68 grooves	60 grooves	46 grooves
Elevation	0 degrees to + 40 degrees	0 degrees to + 40 degrees	0 degrees to + 45 degrees	0 degrees to + 40 degrees
Traverse	2 degrees left and right	2 degrees left and right	240 degrees	360 degrees
Shell	1,134kg (2,500lb) HE shell	567kg (1,250lb)	340kg (750lb) HE shell	172kg (380lb)
Muzzle velocity	573.0m/sec (1,880ft/ sec)	777.2m/sec (2,550ft/sec) 899m/sec (2,950ft/sec) with Supercharge	447.4m/sec (1,468ft/ sec)	640.1m/sec (2,100ft/ sec)
Range	20,391m (12.7 miles)	36,576m (22.7 miles)*	13,122m (8.2 miles)	20,665m (12.8 miles)
Complete	Restored 1940	September 1940 to May 1941	Restored 1939	Restored 1940

* Note: other sources quote 44,700m (27.8 miles) with Supercharge.

BRITISH RAIL GUN 'BOCHE BUSTER'

A number of rail guns were deployed in south-east England at the start of the war, including HMG 'Boche Buster'. This had been used in World War I (albeit with a 14in. gun), but had been mothballed in the interwar years. It was now brought out of retirement and fitted with an 18in. gun. Once the work was completed (at the Darlington rail works near Catterick), it was moved to Kent. The Elham Valley Line, running from Canterbury to Folkestone, was ideally located for rail artillery and was commandeered by the military. The track was upgraded and the gun was stationed in the Bourne Park Tunnel. Magazines were constructed to store shells and steps were added at the southern end of the tunnel to allow easy access to the cutting.

On 13 February 1941, 'Boche Buster' was shunted to the Kingston spur and fired for the first time. The shells landed harmlessly in the Channel but caused considerable damage to nearby properties. Two more test-firings were made, but in spite of its size, the gun had limited range and was little more than a propaganda weapon visited by dignitaries and the Prime Minister. At the end of 1943, with the threat of invasion gone, 'Boche Buster' was withdrawn to Salisbury Plain for firing trials, and after the war was cut up.

gons for shell supply

Bishopsbourne

Bourne Park tunnel

Elham Valley railway line

Kingston Spur

A view of Wanstone No. 1 gun 'Jane' being emplaced in March 1942. The gun weighed more than 100 tonnes, and three cranes were required to gently move the gun into its cradle. One secured the breech, one the trunnions and one the end of the barrel. (Dover Museum)

COASTAL GUNS

'Jane' and 'Clem' (15in.)

The largest fixed guns used by the British were the 15in. Mk 1 guns deployed at Wanstone Farm (Churchill hoped to deploy a 16in. gun, but this idea was shelved). They were mounted in concrete gun pits and were christened 'Jane' (No. 1) and 'Clem' (No. 2), after the eponymous *Daily Mirror* cartoon character and the British Deputy Prime Minister Clement Atlee respectively. (There is an argument that the gun was named after Churchill's wife, Clementine, but she tended to be known as Clemmie. More significantly, Atlee visited Wanstone in May 1942, when the gun was commissioned.) The Mk I had originally been built for the Royal Navy, and although it was of World War I vintage, it was one of the best large-calibre guns ever developed by the British. Five

WANSTONE BATTERY: 15IN. GUN 'JANE'

In September 1940, immediately after 'Winnie', the 14in. gun at St Margaret's at Cliffe, had first fired, the Chiefs of Staff ordered the installation of two further guns on the Kent coast. A suitable location was identified near Wanstone Farm, and the War Office, in the form of the Royal Engineers, was given the task of preparing the sites. The Admiralty was tasked with supplying the guns and the mounts. Vickers Armstrong was contracted to manufacture the mount, which was a slightly modified version of those used in Singapore. Two 15in. guns that were due to be transported to the Far East were redirected to Dover. One was called 'Jane' and was completed in March 1942. The other, some 400m away,

was christened 'Clem' and was completed the following May.

The guns were provided with armoured shields and were heavily camouflaged. Each gun was serviced by a power plant and two magazines to store the shells and charges. The magazines were constructed from reinforced concrete with staggered brick entrances and were located to the rear of each of the positions. The ammunition was moved from the store by small tractors, and then, using a davit, was lifted from the trailer, swung into place and lowered onto a tray that allowed the shell and charge to be loaded. On 13 August 1942, Wanstone fired for the first time; the guns remained operational throughout the war.

Guardroom

Magazine No. 1

Power plant, store, compressor house

Wire

Berm

15in. Gun 'Jane'

Shelter

Nissen huts

Magazine No. 2

railway lines

The breech of the cross-Channel gun 'Winnie' taken in September 1944. A 14in. shell is being lowered into position on a hoist by men of the Royal Marine Siege Regiment. The gun is supporting Canadian troops attacking the German coastal batteries around Calais. (© Imperial War Museum, A25764)

guns had already been installed to protect Singapore, and further barrels were available, in part because of the losses of capital ships suffered by the Royal Navy in the early part of the war (*Royal Oak* in 1939, *Hood* in May 1941 and *Barham* in November 1941). Two more 15in. guns were earmarked for Penang, but in 1940 it was decided to locate them in Kent, and by the spring of 1942 they had been installed. The shore-based guns used a supercharge that increased their range to 38km and typically fired AP shells, because they were more effective than HE against concrete and shipping.

The guns were mounted on a carriage that was pivoted at the front with a semi-circular track or 'race' set in the floor at the rear that allowed them to be traversed; the

14IN. BRITISH COASTAL GUN 'WINNIE'

The first large-calibre gun to be installed on the British mainland was 'Winnie', a 14in. Mk VII gun. This had been designed just before the war for the King George V-class battleships. However, although this was a modern gun, there were worries about using it for extended periods. A spare barrel was made available by the Navy that would need to be installed after the original had fired around 50 rounds. The problem with this was that regularly changing the barrel made it impractical to install the gun in a reinforced concrete bunker. Churchill suggested building a roof from sandbags, which could be removed, but the idea was not adopted. Instead, protection for the gun and crew was provided by an armoured shield and spoil heaped around the gun in berms. Additionally, the position was heavily camouflaged and a dummy gun position was constructed a short distance away to confuse the enemy.

The effectiveness of 'Winnie' was limited by the slowness of loading and the need to conserve ammunition to meet any possible German invasion. Even so, by December 1940 the barrel was worn out and had to be replaced. Cranes, running on rail lines laid to construct the position and move ammunition, removed the old barrel and slotted the new one into the gun cradle.

When 'Jane' and 'Clem' were commissioned, 'Winnie' was put into care and maintenance, but later supported the Canadian attack on Cap Gris-Nez in September 1944.

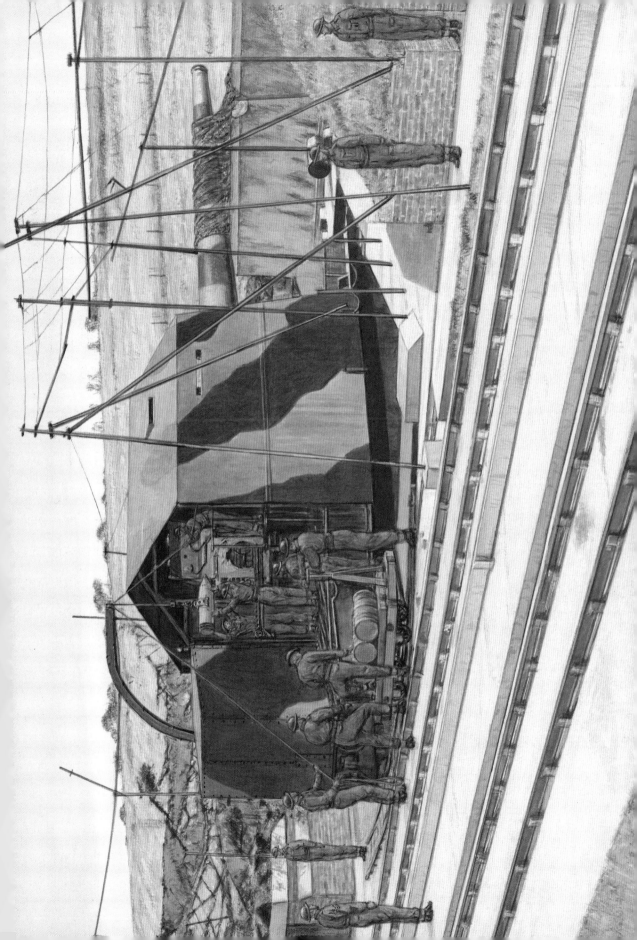

Three cranes manoeuvre the 13.5/8in. high-velocity gun 'Bruce' into place in 1942. Two cranes at the rear share the weight of the breech while a further crane is at the muzzle end. The cranes were provided by Cowans Sheldon and were moved into place on rails. 'Bruce' was initially named 'Wilfred', but this was changed to 'Bruce' after Admiral Sir Bruce Fraser – Controller of the Navy – who had been instrumental in installing 'Winnie' and 'Pooh'. (Dover Museum)

whole was protected by an armoured cab. Shells and the bagged charges were stored in reinforced concrete shelters at the rear.

'Winnie' and 'Pooh'

'Winnie' was a 14in. Mk VII gun, named after Winston Churchill, the new British PM. It was installed by Vickers and was ready by the summer of 1940. Later, another 14in. gun was installed and was christened 'Pooh' (after the A.A. Milne character) that was ready early in 1941. (It is interesting to note at this point that British guns tended to have light-hearted names like 'Winnie', 'Pooh', 'Jane' and 'Clem' whereas the German guns were more martial: 'Anton', 'Bruno', 'Cäsar' etc.) The guns were mounted on specially adapted navy gun cradles. One of them had been moved from the training range at Shoeburyness, where it had been used to test one of the massive 18in. guns that were fitted to 'Boche Buster'. The cradles were in turn mounted on a turntable that allowed the gun to traverse. The shells for the 14in. guns were supplied with a supercharge which allowed them to fire 46km. However, with no effective fire control, they could not engage ships in the Channel.

The need to regularly change the barrels meant that it was not possible to install the guns in a concrete shelter. Instead, an armoured cab was prefabricated to protect the gun and crew. Shells and charges were stored away from the gun position in brick and concrete shelters with an overhead rail that allowed the shells to be retrieved. The shells and charges were moved by rail to the gun position. A davit with grabber enabled the crew to move the shell from the trolley to the breech.

'Bruce'

The development of aircraft that could carry bombs all but killed off the development of long-range guns, but not completely. Churchill's scientific advisor Frederick Lindemann, a prolific innovator, suggested the idea of a hypervelocity gun. Three 13.5in. Mk V guns (the same barrel as used by the rail guns) were relined to 8in. and

A view of No. 2 gun of South Foreland Battery taken in March 1942. The gun has been camouflaged and the area around the gun pit neatly landscaped. The picture was taken soon after the Channel Dash, when the battery unsuccessfully engaged three large German warships. (Royal Artillery Museum)

one of these was installed on a special mount in a prepared concrete position near St Margaret's at Cliffe in January 1943. The gun was World War I vintage, but the shells were modern, custom-made with external rifling, or splines, that matched that of the gun. This created a tighter fit, but also necessitated a bespoke tool to ram the projectiles, which significantly slowed the rate of fire.

The gun was first test-fired in June 1942 at Grain Island Firing Point, Yantlet Creek; when fully installed, further experimental firing took place in March 1943 and continued into 1944. The performance of the weapon was extraordinary, firing a 116kg shell over 100km. However, the stress on the barrel was such that after firing only a few rounds the rifling was badly eroded. It took two weeks to replace the barrel/liner and meant that it was not practical to employ the weapon. It was taken out of service in February 1945. The naval historian John Campbell concluded that 'Bruce' was 'not [a] very successful super-velocity gun – a remarkable waste of effort.'

South Foreland Battery

Work began on the South Foreland position at the end of 1940, and by January 1942 all four guns were ready for action. The position was armed with 9.2in. Mk 10 guns. The gun had been developed at the end of the 19th century and was adopted by both the Army and the Navy. The guns were used on battleships and cruisers, and when these ships were decommissioned, some of the guns were converted for use on shore (and as rail guns). They were the principal weapon for coastal defence at the start of World War II.

The guns at South Foreland were installed in an open pit on a Mk 5c mounting. The gun itself was protected by a steel shield and roof. The shells and cordite charges were stored in reinforced concrete magazines immediately behind the gun positions.

The four guns were given unofficial names:

No. 1 Shoeburyness – after the firing range in Essex;

No. 2 Prinz Eugen (after the German ship that slipped through the Channel in February 1942);

No. 3 Gneisenau (ditto);

No. 4 Scharnhorst (ditto).

Table 3: British coastal guns				
	'Clem' and 'Jane' 15in. Mk 1 (38.1cm)	'Winnie' and 'Pooh' 14In. Mk 7 (35.6cm)	'Bruce' 13.5/8in. (34.3/20.3cm)	South Foreland 9.2in. Mk 10 (23.4cm)
Weight (gun/breech)	101,605kg (224,000lb)	80,865kg (178,276lb)	86,974kg (191,743lb)	28,450kg (62,720lb)
Total weight	378,987kg (373 tons)	?	203,210kg (200 tons) approx.	127,006kg (125 tons)
Length of bore	16.002m (630.0in.) 42-cal.	16.002m (630in.) 45-cal.	18.313m (721in.) 90-cal.	10.905m (429in.) 46.7-cal.
Length	16.520m (650.4in.)	16.532m (650.85in.)	18.804m (740.3in.)	11.236m (442.4in.)
Rifling	76 grooves	72 grooves	16 grooves	37 grooves
Elevation	-2 degrees to +45 degrees	0 degrees to +55 degrees	-7 degrees to +50 degrees	-5 degrees to +35 degrees
Traverse	240 degrees	130 degrees	140 degrees	360 degrees
Shell	879kg (1,938lb) APC	719kg (1,586lb)	116kg (256lb)	172kg (380lb)
Rate of fire	2rpm	2rpm	?	2–3rpm
Muzzle velocity	731.5m/sec (2,400ft/sec) 816.9m/sec (2,680ft/sec) with supercharge	756.8m/sec (2,483ft/sec) 868.7m/sec (2,850ft/sec) with supercharge	1,402.1m/sec (4,600ft/sec)	837.6m/sec (2,748ft/sec) 875.4m/sec (2,872ft/sec) with supercharge
Range	33,741m (c. 21 miles) 38,405m (24 miles) with supercharge	46,630m (c. 29 miles) with supercharge	100,584m (c. 62.5 miles)	26,700m (16.6 miles) 33,560m (20.9 miles) with supercharge
Complete	March 1942 ('Jane') and May 1942 ('Clem')	August 1940 ('Winnie') and February 1941 ('Pooh')	March 1943	July 1941 to January 1942

GERMAN

RAIL GUNS

21cm K12 (E)

Two 21cm Kanone 12 Eisenbahn were built by Krupp and each was different. The first weapon – K12 V (E) – was delivered to the Army in March 1939. The barrel was fitted with trunnions and mounted on a gondola that sat across two smaller carriages. The carriage at the front had two bogies with five axles each and the rear carriage had two bogies each with four axles.

The gun was 33.3m long and could fire a shell 115km (although the furthest it is recorded as firing is 88km). The lining lasted 100–150 rounds before it needed to be replaced. The soft-metal ribs on the shell meant that even as the rifling deteriorated, there was no loss of pressure and as such no reduction of range or accuracy. The barrel weighed 100 tonnes and was so heavy that it had to be braced along its length to stop it bending under its own weight. The breech block was similarly massive and acted as a counterweight.

A hydraulic jacking system was needed to raise the gun off the ground to ensure the breech did not hit the ground when firing. To reload the gun the jacks had to be lowered, which was slow and cumbersome and was far from ideal in a war situation. A new gun was produced that dispensed with the jacks and used hydro-pneumatic balancing presses. The new gun, which also had a different axle set-up, was delivered in mid-1940 and was called the K12 N (E).

28cm K5 (E)

The 28cm Kanone 5 Eisenbahn was also developed by Krupp, but was much simpler than the K12 and was produced in greater numbers – between 1936 and the end of the war 28 were manufactured. The 28cm rifled barrel was a third shorter than the K12, which meant it did not need to be braced, nor did it need to be raised off the ground to fire. The barrel was trunnioned to the carriage, which was mounted on two sets of bogies each with six axles (12 wheels). Like the K12, the K5 had limited traverse and relied on curved sections of track, a 'T' section of track or a Vögele turntable to extend its arc of fire – the latter giving the gun full 360-degree traverse. Firing a standard shell, the K5 had a range of a shade over 60km – significantly less than the K12 – but it could comfortably hit targets in south-east England and the payload was far greater.

Table 4: German rail guns		
	K12 V (E) 21cm	K5 28cm
Manufacturer	Friedrich Krupp AG, Essen	Friedrich Krupp AG, Essen
Weight (gun/breech)	99,800kg 99,700kg for K12 N	83,000kg
Weight (travel)	309,000kg	218,000kg
Weight (firing)	317,000kg 318,000kg for K12 N	210,000kg
Length of barrel	33,300mm L/158	21,500mm L/76
Rifling	Eight grooves	12 grooves
Breech mechanism	Horizontal sliding breech block	Horizontal sliding breech block
Elevation	up to +55 degrees	up to +50 degrees
Traverse	14' or 0.23 degrees (360 degrees on turntable)	18' or 0.3 degrees (360 degrees on turntable)
Shell	107.5kg	255kg
Rate of fire	One every 5 mins	One every 3–5 mins
Muzzle	1,625m/sec	1,120m/sec
Range	115km	62km
Length of carriage	41,300mm (including carriages)	31,100mm (including carriages)
Number of axles	20 axles (4 bogies x 5 axles) K12 N (E) – 18 axles (2 bogies x 5 axles and 2 bogies x 4 axles)	2 bogies x 6 axles
Complete	1938	1936

One of the reinforced concrete observation posts that was constructed as part of Stützpunkt 139 'Hamm' which was used by the Germans to direct the cross-Channel guns. The position was located just inland from Wissant on Mont de Couple. This was one of the highest pieces of ground in the area, from which there was an uninterrupted view of the Channel and the White Cliffs beyond. (Author's photograph)

COASTAL GUNS

'Lindemann'

The largest cross-Channel guns were the 40.6cm (16in.) guns mounted at Marine-Küsten-Batterie 'Lindemann'. The guns had originally been designed for the German 'H'-class battleship, which was cancelled at the start of the war. It is believed that as many as 12 of these guns had been completed before it was decided to cancel production and use them for coastal defence. Seven were modified and were deployed in Norway. (The coastal version of this gun had a larger chamber and was called 'Adolf'.) Three unmodified guns were installed in the Hel Fortified Area, Poland as Batterie Schleswig-Holstein during 1940. They were all fired during May and June 1941, before being dismantled and transported to France. The gun battery was initially christened 'Grossdeutschland', but was renamed 'Lindemann' in honour of the late Kapitän zur See Ernst Lindemann, the commander of battleship *Bismarck*, which was sunk in May 1941. Each turret had a name – 'Anton', 'Bruno' and 'Cäsar'.

GERMAN K12 RAIL GUN, STÜTZPUNKT 192 'BISMARCK'

The 21cm K12 E railway gun was based on the Paris guns which had been used to bombard the French capital in 1918. The first of these guns – the K12 V – was test-fired in 1936 and delivered to the German Army in 1939. A second simpler design – the K12 N – was delivered in 1940. The K12s had no fire control system, so they were only suited to hitting large targets like Dover and Folkestone, but the 115km range meant they could also hit the towns of Thanet.

Both guns were eventually allocated to Eisenbahn-Batterie 701 and were deployed to Stützpunkt 192 'Bismarck' at Hydrequent. Here, a mixture of reinforced concrete bunkers and tunnels bored into the cliff provided protection against any Allied bombing. The site was provided with Vögele turntables, which allowed the guns to traverse.

At the end of the war, a K12 gun was captured by Allied forces in the Netherlands. They were impressed with the weapon, but it was now considered outdated and of little military use.

Tunnel No. 1

Tunnel No. 2

rail lines

Cliff face

The guns were mounted on the Bettungsschiessgerüst (platform firing framework) C/39. Bogies at the rear that ran on a rail track enabled the whole turret to rotate. Initially, the gun was only protected by the armoured turret, but later a concrete casemate was constructed. The shells and charges were stored in four underground magazines and were moved by hoist to the rear of the turret and then by trolley to the breech. Traverse and elevation were powered, but ramming was manual. The gun barrel was fitted with a liner, which was changed after 180–210 rounds.

Turret 4 of Batterie 'Todt' as it stands today. The structure is in a good state of repair. The gun was removed by the French just after the war and sent to the arsenal at Ruelle to be refurbished. The plan was to install a smaller-calibre gun, but nothing came of this plan. (Author's photograph)

'Todt'

Perhaps the best known of the cross-Channel batteries was Marine-Küsten-Batterie 'Todt'. The position was originally christened 'Siegfried', but it was renamed in honour of the German engineer Fritz Todt, creator of the Organisation Todt, who died in an air crash on 8 February 1942.

The four 38cm SK C/34 naval guns that were installed at Haringzelle were originally planned for the Bismarck-class battleships. Two of these were completed – *Bismarck* and *Tirpitz* – before production was cancelled. As well as the HE and AP shells developed for the Kriegsmarine, one was developed for the Wehrmacht – a special long-range shell known as the 'Siegfried Granate', which considerably increased the range of the guns. The barrel was fitted with a loose liner that was removed from the breech end and had to be changed after 180–210 rounds. However, with the lighter coastal 'Siegfried' artillery shell, barrel life increased to around 350 rounds.

Work began on the position in August 1940 and was completed in November 1941. The guns were initially installed in open concrete barbettes, with protection for the crew provided by their turret armour. However, the proximity of the battery to Britain meant it was vulnerable to shelling and bombing, and Hitler ordered the construction of concrete casemates to protect the guns. The reinforced concrete walls

and roof were 3.5m thick and able to resist 38cm shells, but did restrict the traverse to 120 degrees. The newly reinforced battery was inaugurated in February 1942.

Each casemate consisted of two parts: the firing chamber, which housed the gun mounted on a pedestal under an armoured turret; and, on two floors (one of which was underground), the ammunition magazines and all the space needed for the machinery and the crew.

'Friedrich August'

Following the defeat of France, three 30.5cm SK L/50 guns were installed at La Trésorerie, near Boulogne-sur-Mer, where they assumed their former name of Batterie 'Friedrich August' (from their time on the island of Wangerooge in the North Sea). These guns were initially in open barbettes with 360-degree traverse, but later concrete casemates were constructed to provide overhead cover.

The turret was organized over two levels, with the gun and loading gear on the upper floor and the ammunition hoist, traversing and elevation gear on the lower level. The ammunition was stored in an underground magazine at the rear of the concrete shelter and was moved by trolleys to the handling room. From here hoists took the ammunition to the lower-level compartment. A lighter shell was developed for the gun, which increased the range and extended barrel life to approximately 200 rounds.

Private F.J. Coakley of The North Shore Regiment sitting on one of the 30.5cm SK L/50 guns of Batterie 'Friedrich August'. The three naval guns were manned by men of Marine-Artillerie-Abteilung 240. The gun was located near Boulogne, France and was captured on 19 September 1944. (Lieutenant Donald I. Grant/Library and Archives Canada/Department of National Defence, PA167981)

To the south of the main gun positions of Batterie 'Grosser Kurfürst' is a large reserve ammunition store that was capable of storing 300 rounds for the 28cm guns. (Author's photograph)

'Grosser Kurfürst'

One of the first batteries to be installed was Marine-Küsten-Batterie 'Grosser Kurfürst', which was located to the rear of Cap Gris-Nez near Framzelle. The four 28cm SK L/50 guns were initially installed in open pits, but later were mounted on S412 reinforced concrete shelters.

'Prinz Heinrich'

In July 1940, two 28cm SK L/45 guns were mounted in open emplacements near Sangatte, and were the first large-calibre guns to be installed to support the planned invasion of Britain. It was christened Marine-Küsten-Batterie 'Prinz Heinrich' after Gross Admiral Albert Wilhelm Heinrich, Prinz von Preussen. The 28cm SK L/45 gun had been developed by the German Navy before World War I and was mounted on

MARINE-KÜSTEN-BATTERIE 'GROSSER KURFÜRST'

In June 1940, the Germans began work to install guns near the village of Framzelle on Cap Gris-Nez. This position became known as Batterie 'Grosser Kurfürst' (Great Elector) and was initially armed with 28cm SK L/45 guns in an open barbette. In August, the battery fired for the first time and by the end of the year had fired 451 shells. Later, a decision was taken to replace the L/45s with the more powerful 28cm SK L/50 gun, which was capable of firing a shell 39km. (Seven 28cm SK L/50s had been used for coastal defence at Pillau, now Baltiysk, East Prussia. These were removed and three were installed in Norway and four at Cap Gris-Nez.) Four S412 bunkers (shown here) were constructed to accommodate the new guns and the C/37 mount.

The guns were protected with 6cm-thick armoured turrets, which were strengthened with additional appliqué armour. This was not impervious to Allied bombs and shells, but meant that the guns were able to rotate 360 degrees. In October 1941, the first SK L/50 gun was ready for use, and all four had been completed by April 1942. The battery continued to operate throughout the war, but over time the performance of the guns diminished and, unable to replace the barrels, the range of the weapons declined to 26km by September 1944 – insufficient to reach the British coast.

Supporting each gun emplacement were two ammunition bunkers and two personnel bunkers (each one named after famous German military leaders or naval victories). In addition, there was a kitchen, hospital, machine room and water tank. Protecting the whole position were a series of Tobruks, Michelmannstands (small open concrete shelters), 5cm gun pits as well as Flak and Pak positions.

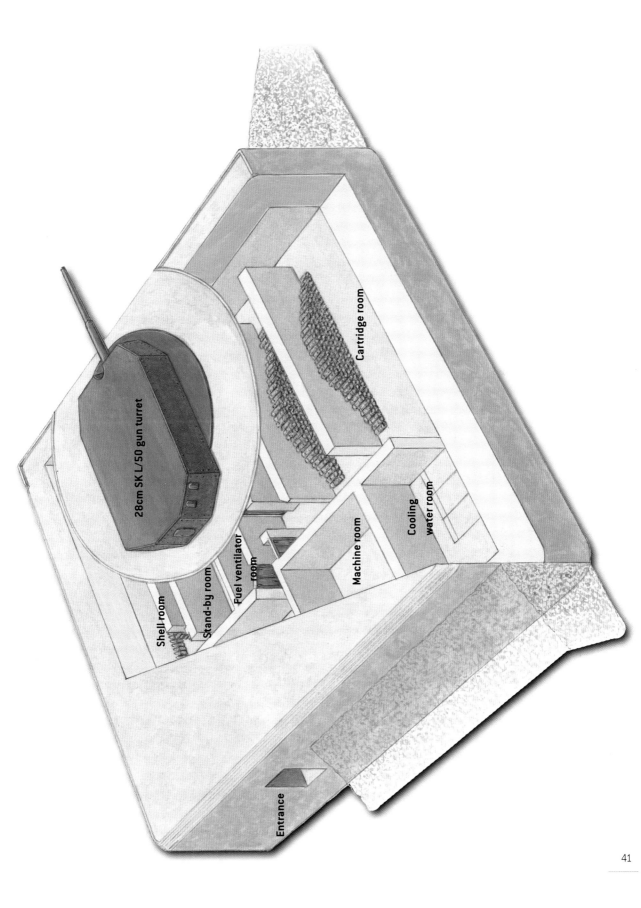

28cm SK L/50 gun turret

Shell room

Stand-by room

Fuel ventilator room

Cartridge room

Machine room

Cooling water room

Entrance

Batterie 'Prinz Heinrich' was the first battery to be established on the Channel coast in the summer of 1940. In 1943, the battery was transferred to Leningrad and replaced by Batterie 'Grosser Kurfürst'. This ammunition storage room serviced the 28cm guns. (Author's photograph)

the first German dreadnoughts. Later, the guns were used as coast artillery. Two guns were installed at Fehmarn, an island in the Baltic Sea, before being moved to the Channel coast. To increase their range, they were supplied with a lighter shell with a larger propellant charge.

In April 1943, after the plan to invade Britain had been abandoned, the guns were moved to Leningrad to support the siege of the city. The gap left by the battery was filled by the renovated Batterie 'Grosser Kurfürst'.

'Oldenburg'

Marine-Küsten-Batterie 'Oldenburg' (colloquially known as 'le Moulin Rouge') was constructed just outside Calais. Initially, the two guns were installed in open positions. However, in the autumn of 1940 work began on the construction of concrete bunkers to protect the guns.

The battery was armed with two Russian 10in. (25.4cm) guns captured by the Germans in 1915. The guns were re-chambered by Krupp to 24cm so that they could use existing German ammunition (for the 24cm SK L/40) and were converted to a horizontal breech mechanism. The gun was redesignated as the 24cm SK L/50. Although they used a standard 24cm shell, a different propellant charge was used that increased the muzzle velocity and the range.

The battery consisted of two casemates – Turm Ost (East) or 'Borkum', and Turm West or 'Ösel'. The former was constructed over three storeys. The gun was mounted at ground level with ammunition rooms. Below this were the crew quarters and in the basement was the machine room. Turm West was constructed over two levels – the machine room was located in a separate bunker.

Batterie 'Oldenburg' near Calais consisted of two large casemates each mounting a 24cm gun. The position is still in remarkably good shape, as demonstrated here by the eastern casemate. A walkway at the rear takes you from the road to the first casemate. The aperture has been fenced off. (Author's photograph)

Table 5: German coastal guns

	'Lindemann' 40.6cm SK C/34	'Todt' 38cm SK C/34	'Friedrich August' 30.5cm SK L/50	'Grosser Kurfürst' 28cm SK L/50	'Prinz Heinrich' 28cm SK L/45	'Oldenburg' 24cm SK L/50
Original name	Schleswig-Holstein (at Hel) Grossdeutschland	Siegfried				
Original location	Hel, seized by Germany from Poland in 1939		Wangerooge, Frisian Island, Germany then installed in West Wall	Pillau, East Prussia, Germany	Fehmarn, Baltic, Germany	Borkum, Frisian Island, Germany then installed in West Wall
Location	Sangatte, Cap Blanc-Nez	Haringzelle, Cap Gris-Nez	La Trésorerie, Boulogne	Framzelle, Cap Gris-Nez	Sangatte	Calais
Alternative name	Stp 107 Neuss	Stp 166 Saitenspiel (Alt Stp 213)	Stp Kornweihe 212	Stp 155 Tümmler (1944) [Alt Stp 17 (1941) then Stp 211 Dummkopf (1942)]	Stp 125	Stp 18
Number of guns	3	4	3	4	2	2
Weight (gun/breech)	158,660kg	105,300kg	51,850kg	41,500kg	39,800kg	unknown
Length	20,300mm (L/50)	19,630mm (L/52)	15,250mm (L/50)	14,150mm (L/50)	12,735mm (L/45)	11,900mm (L/5C)
Rifling	110 grooves	90 grooves	88 grooves	80 grooves	80 grooves	n/a
Traverse	120 degrees in casemate	120 degrees in casemate	120 degrees in casemate	360 degrees	360 degrees	120 degrees in casemate
Shell	1,030kg (standard) 600kg (long range)	495kg (long range 'Siegfried') 800kg (heavy)	250kg (HE shell) 405kg (APHE)	284kg	284kg	148.5kg
Rate of fire	1–2 rpm	2–3 rpm	2–3 rpm	2–3 rpm	unknown	unknown
Muzzle velocity	810m/sec (standard) 1,050m/sec (long-range shell)	820m/sec (heavy shell) 1,050m/sec (long-range 'Siegfried')	855m/sec (APHE shell) 1,120m/sec (HE shell)	895m/sec	875m/sec	700m/sec
Range	42,800m (standard) 56,000m (long range)	42,000m (heavy shell) 55,700m (long-range 'Siegfried')	32,500m (APHE) 51,000m (HE shell)	39,100m	36,100m	26,700m
Complete	1942	1940	1940	1941	1940	1941
Manufacturer	Friedrich Krupp AG, Essen	Friedrich Krupp AG, Essen	Friedrich Krupp AG, Essen and Skoda, Pilsen under licence	Friedrich Krupp AG, Essen	Friedrich Krupp AG, Essen	Russian gun adapted by Krupp
Mount	Bettungsschiessgerüst C/39	Bettungsschiessgerüst C/39	Bettungsschiessgerüst C/40	Küsten-Drehscheiben-Lafette C/37	Küsten-Drehscheiben-Lafette C/37	unknown

THE COMBATANTS

BRITISH

At the turn of the 20th century, coastal artillery was the responsibility of the Royal Garrison Artillery (RGA). However, in the interwar period, as the Army looked to save money, the RGA was absorbed into the Royal Artillery (RA) and coastal artillery was given over to the Territorial Army (TA) – a part-time volunteer force of the British Army. Following the declaration of war in September 1939, the TA was mobilized and the Royal Artillery Heavy Regiments were ordered to man the guns around the coast. In the south-east, the Kent and Sussex Heavy Regiment RA (TA) was charged with manning the coastal guns of Dover and Newhaven under Dover Fire Command.

During the Phoney War, some minor changes were made to coastal defences. In December 1939, the Coast Artillery took over responsibility for operating searchlights from the Fortress Royal Engineers. The most seismic change came after the Dunkirk evacuation and the defeat of France in June 1940. An assortment of naval guns was released from store to defend ports and possible landing sites. These 'Emergency Coast Batteries' were manned by the Royal Navy. However, the senior service could not support land-based operations indefinitely; men were needed to crew naval vessels. Coast Artillery would need to man the batteries. Officers were called up from the reserves, NCOs were combed out of training units and gunners were recruited from the Royal Artillery regiments that been evacuated from Dunkirk (and who had lost their heavy equipment) while others were fast-tracked through training.

This rapid increase in the size and spread of the Coast Artillery also necessitated a restructuring. Batteries were grouped into regiments under a lieutenant-colonel and the role of Commander Corps Coast Artillery (CCCA) was established under a

Brigadier. CCCA Dover was established in June 1940 under Brigadier C.W. Raw RA. Initially he commanded nos. 519, 520 and 521 (Kent and Sussex) Coast regiments, which were established in July 1940.

In September 1940, three further batteries were planned: Fan Bay, South Foreland and Wanstone. Initially, these batteries were under Eastern Counter Bombardment Fire Command commanded by Major Shrive (from November 1940 acting lieutenant-colonel). In December 1940, this command was redesignated as 540 Coast Regiment RA. In October 1941, Shrive retired (he was 50), but was reinstated and continued in this role. In January 1942, Lieutenant-Colonel J.H.W.G. Richards took over command of 540 Coast Regiment. Richards had previously been the principal instructor at 73 Coast Training Regiment based at Pembroke Dock, and when he moved to Kent, he took with him a number of his most trusted officers.

Brigadier Raw, as CCCA Dover, reported to Lieutenant-General Andrew Thorne (GOC XII Corps) who in turn reported to Commander-in-Chief, Home Forces (from May to July 1940, this was General Sir Edmund Ironside; he was replaced by General Sir Alan Brooke, who held the role until December 1941). In April 1941, Thorne moved on and was replaced by a certain Lieutenant-General Bernard Montgomery, who was GOC until November 1941. Brigadier Burrowes – GSO(1) Eastern Command – was responsible for coastal artillery at XII Corps HQ, and a battery was to be named after him, but was eventually christened 'Hougham'.

Men of 540 Coast Regiment RA in 1943, possibly in the garden of South Foreland Lighthouse. Back row, left to right: Major R. Lineham MBE, MM (Quartermaster), Lieutenant Snowden, Lieutenant (later Major) W. Eaton (OC Fan Bay Battery), Lieutenant Higgs, Lieutenant (later Captain) A.L. Strange (took over Fan Bay in August 1944), unknown, unknown, Major H. Philpots DCM (Armament Officer). Front row, left to right: Church of England chaplain, Major E.D. Hagger (OC South Foreland Battery), Major Kenyon (2inC), Lieutenant-Colonel J.H.W.G. Richards (OinC), Major E.B. Edmonds (OC Wanstone Battery), Captain (later Major) R.F.A. Mallinson, Lieutenant (later Captain) A. Boardman. (Royal Artillery Museum)

Table 6: Major batteries in and around Dover

Battery	Calibre	No. of guns	Command	Regiment	Battery	Notes
Citadel	9.2in. (pre-war)	2	Western Counter Bombardment (CB) Fire Command**	520	295	Originally three guns
Hougham	8in.	3		520	428	Installed September 1942
Capel*	8in.	3		520	424	Installed May 1942
Lydden Spout	6in.	3		520	423	Installed May 1941
Wanstone	15in.	2	Eastern CB Fire Command	540	302	4 x 5.5in. guns installed September 1940 at St Margaret's Bay
Fan Bay	6in.	3			203	
South Foreland	9.2in.	4			290	
'Winnie' and 'Pooh'	14in.	2		Royal Marine Siege Regiment (RMSR)		
'Bruce'	8in.	1		RMSR		

Notes:

* Capel Battery replaced Abbots Battery. The Navy confirmed that the original site was no longer available for Coastal Artillery, so a new site (Capel) had to be found.

** In December 1940, this became 520 Coast Regiment and from 1941 was commanded by Lieutenant-Colonel McLernon.

Alongside the smaller-calibre emergency batteries, Churchill ordered heavy artillery to be deployed to the coast. Large rail guns were moved to the south-east and work started on one and then two 14in. gun positions. With one notable exception, these large-calibre guns were placed under the command of the Royal Marine Siege Regiment. The regiment was made up of two batteries (as well as a Spotter Balloon section and AA guns). 'A' Battery consisted of three troops (nos. 1, 2 and 6) that manned the 14in. guns 'Winnie' and 'Pooh' and also the 8in. gun 'Bruce'. 'B' Battery was also made up of three troops (nos. 3, 4 and 5) and was responsible for the 13.5in. railway guns ('Piecemaker', 'Scene Shifter' and 'Gladiator'). In early July 1940, Acting Lieutenant-Colonel H.D. Fellowes arrived at St Margaret's at Cliffe to take command. From 20 April 1941, the RMSR was administered by the Commander Royal Artillery (CRA) of XII Corps. In November 1943, responsibility for the rail guns passed to the Royal Artillery when they were withdrawn from the coast.

The one exception was the 18in. rail gun 'Boche Buster'. This was manned by 80 officers and men of the 11th Super Heavy Battery from the 2nd Super Heavy Regiment of the Royal Artillery, which also formed part of XII Corps.

CONSTRUCTION

A series of conferences were convened in the second half of 1940 to consider the siting of new gun batteries and their relative priority. At these conferences, chaired by CinC

Home Forces, it was decided to construct seven batteries. The recommendations were considered and agreed by the War Office Siting Board, chaired by Major-General F.W. Barron (Inspector Field Defences). Interestingly, on 3 September 1940 CinC Home Forces agreed to install guns at South Foreland. Later that month, the War Office Siting Board agreed to install four guns (rather than three), but this meant putting them closer together. However, South Foreland had been given a lower priority than other batteries and the resulting shortages of men and materials caused delays to construction.

The batteries were constructed by a mixture of civilian and military manpower. So, for example, the gun emplacements and engine rooms for South Foreland were built by Richard Costain Ltd, a civilian construction firm. The accommodation was the responsibility of 702 Constructional Company, part of the Royal Engineers. The Royal Engineers also deployed one of its tunnelling companies – 172 Tunnelling Company – which had been established in World War I for mining. In November 1940, the company moved to Dover and began work on shelters for troops manning the various batteries, including those at South Foreland. The work was completed by March 1941 and the 'moles' moved to Wanstone, where they constructed the Battery Plotting Room (BPR) and Fortress Plotting Room (FPR).

A picture taken in July 1941 of No. 4 gun of South Foreland Battery. The wooden shuttering was used as a formwork for the concrete to be poured. The doors in the foreground allowed the workers to get access to the gun pit. The site was also visited by Anthony Gross, the war artist, who captured the same image in 'Constructing a Gun Emplacement' (Imperial War Museum ART LD 1112). (Royal Artillery Museum)

WINSTON CHURCHILL

Churchill became the British PM on 10 May 1940 – the same day that Germany invaded France and the Low Countries. Soon after, he visited Kent and was dismayed to see German shipping using the Channel seemingly with impunity. He asked Vice Admiral Bertram Ramsay, CinC Dover, why the enemy vessels were not being engaged, and was informed that there were no shore batteries with the range to hit them. Churchill immediately ordered that large-calibre guns – both fixed and mobile – be deployed along the coast.

On 5 June 1940, Churchill asked for half a dozen 15in. guns to be installed. The First Sea Lord (Admiral Sir Dudley Pound) explained that this would not be feasible, but it would be possible to mount a 14in. gun. On 21 June, Churchill wrote to General Ismay: 'Don't let this matter sleep. Our guns must fire as soon as theirs.' From intelligence reports Churchill was aware that the Germans were installing large-gun batteries on the French coast as a precursor to an invasion. On 3 August, Churchill wrote again to Ismay: 'The 14in. gun I ordered to be mounted at Dover should be ready in ample time to deal with this new German battery.' And it was.

On 22 August, German heavy coastal guns shelled Dover, and 'Winnie', the 14in. coastal gun and his namesake, retaliated. This was commendable, but Churchill was not satisfied. In that same month, although the United States had not entered the war, Churchill tried to purchase 16in. guns from them to mount on the coast. This came to nought, but Churchill was determined to slow or stop the work on the enemy gun positions. On 25 August, he wrote to the First Sea Lord about the possibility of HMS *Erebus* firing on Cap Gris-Nez. Churchill recalled the role played by the monitor in World War I when it shelled Zeebrugge and Ostend. He wanted *Erebus* to again be used to shell German positions on the Continent. In a letter to General Ismay and the First Sea Lord on 31 August 1940, Churchill stressed the urgency of attacking the batteries on the French coast: 'Yesterday's photographs show guns being actually hoisted up into position, and it will be wise to fire on them before they are able to reply' (W. Churchill, *The Second World War*, Vol. 2: *Their Finest Hour*, Penguin Books, London, 1985, p. 244).

The following day he wrote to the First Lord of the Admiralty and First Sea Lord: 'I am deeply concerned at your news that you cannot attack these batteries … until the 16th [of September]. You are allowing an artillery concentration to be developed day after day which presently will forbid the entry of all British ships into the Straits of Dover' (ibid. p. 589).

Churchill's interest was not confined to the technical aspects of the coastal guns. He was very aware of the power of propaganda and went to see the defences in Kent on a number of occasions. On 12 September 1940, he visited 'Winnie'. He also visited the railway gun HMG 'Boche Buster', and, in January 1941, the 15in. guns at Wanstone, though they were not ready for action.

HMG 'Boche Buster' was an 18in. rail gun that was moved to Kent in 1941. Though massive, the rail gun had a limited range, but was a valuable propaganda weapon. Churchill visited it in June 1941.
(© Imperial War Museum, H10870)

Between the beach and the D940 road, set just below Batterie 'Lindemann', is an Organisation Todt cemetery. It is unspectacular, with a small inscription '*1941 ERBAUT DURCH DIE ORG TODT ENTWURF U AUSFÜHRUNG KURZ UND MÜLLER*' – literally, '1941 built by Org Todt Design and Construction Kurz and Müller'. (Author's photograph)

GERMAN

ORGANISATION TODT

The Organisation Todt (OT), named after its founder Dr Fritz Todt, was the organization responsible for civil and military construction in the Third Reich. It was instrumental in the construction of the *Autobahnen*, but increasingly its focus changed and soon it had been given responsibility for completing the West Wall – the German defences along the border with France.

When Germany went to war, this shift continued, and the OT became a *Wehrmachtsgefolge* or Army Auxiliary. In this role, it supported the Army in the West by repairing roads and bridges to ensure continuity of supply. With the defeat of France in June 1940, the OT was put to work building defences on the coast. This included the construction of the large coastal batteries. Work on these positions began almost immediately. OT workers (some from defeated countries) were paid, but increasingly the OT was supplemented by forced labour, including POWs.

The OT was responsible for all facets of construction including:

- All building materials (save for specialist items);
- The labour force, including their security and accommodation;
- Machinery; and
- Quality of the work.

An OT headquarters was established in Paris – OT Gruppe West, which commanded a series of *Einsätze* including Einsatz Kanalküste (Deployment Channel

OT heirarchy from *Oberbauleitungen* down to *Baustellen*.

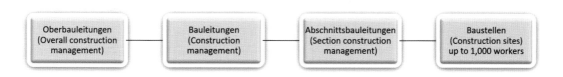

| Oberbauleitungen (Overall construction management) | → | Bauleitungen (Construction management) | → | Abschnittsbauleitungen (Section construction management) | → | Baustellen (Construction sites) up to 1,000 workers |

49

Coast). Under this command were a series of *Oberbauleitungen* including Oberbauleitung Audinghen, which was responsible for the large coastal batteries.

FESTUNGSPIONIERE

With the defeat of France, the Kriegsmarine was made responsible for constructing naval batteries on the Channel coast. To facilitate this work *Festungspioniere* (Fortress Engineers) were assigned to provide technical and tactical support. Specifically:

- Identifying the sites;
- Designs for the defences;
- Providing work schedules and technical drawings for the OT;
- Provision of specialist fittings including:
  - Weapons;
  - Electrics;
  - Heating;
  - Water and sewage;
  - Ventilation; and
  - Final fitting out (beds etc.)
- Final commissioning into service.

Initially, the fortress engineers were divided into five *Festungsbaustäbe* (Fortress Construction Staff). Festungsbaustab Kanalküste was further divided into two, with Festungsbaustab Calais responsible for the oversight of the cross-Channel batteries. Subordinate to this staff was Marinebaubataillon (Naval Construction Battalion) 360 which had completed work on both Batterie 'Prinz Heinrich' and 'Grosser Kurfürst' by the end of July 1940. In the following months, the scale and scope of the construction programme grew and prompted a number of reorganizations, such that

STÜTZPUNKT 89 'FULDA' RAIL GUN BUNKER

Following the defeat of France in 1940, German rail guns were moved to the coast to support a cross-Channel invasion of Britain. Initially, they were housed in rail tunnels and, with limited traverse, used curves in the tracks to engage different targets. After a brief interlude supporting Operation *Barbarossa*, a number of rail guns were returned to France, where a series of bespoke positions were constructed. One of these positions was Stützpunkt 89 'Fulda' (Calais Nieulay) where Eisenbahn-Batterie 710 was located with its two 28cm K5 rail guns. (Originally, this strongpoint was called Stützpunkt 151 'Feige', but in June 1944 it was renamed.)

The site had a reinforced concrete bunker that could house two rail guns and was known as a Dombunker – 'cathedral' or 'dome' bunker. It was constructed in a long cigar shape, typically 80m long and 10m high, and was capable of withstanding all but the largest Allied bombs – the ovoid shape helping to deflect the ordnance. To give the guns a full 360-degree capability, the Germans developed the Vögele turntable. This was easy to produce, transport (it could be loaded onto a railway flatbed car) and erect (in 48 hours).

Ammunition for the guns was stored in reinforced concrete bunkers near the turntables. These were compartmentalized and had an overhead track system to allow the easy movement of shells and charges. Reinforced concrete bunkers were also constructed to house the crew and to act as a command post/HQ. The whole position was protected by anti-aircraft and anti-tank guns and artillery pieces.

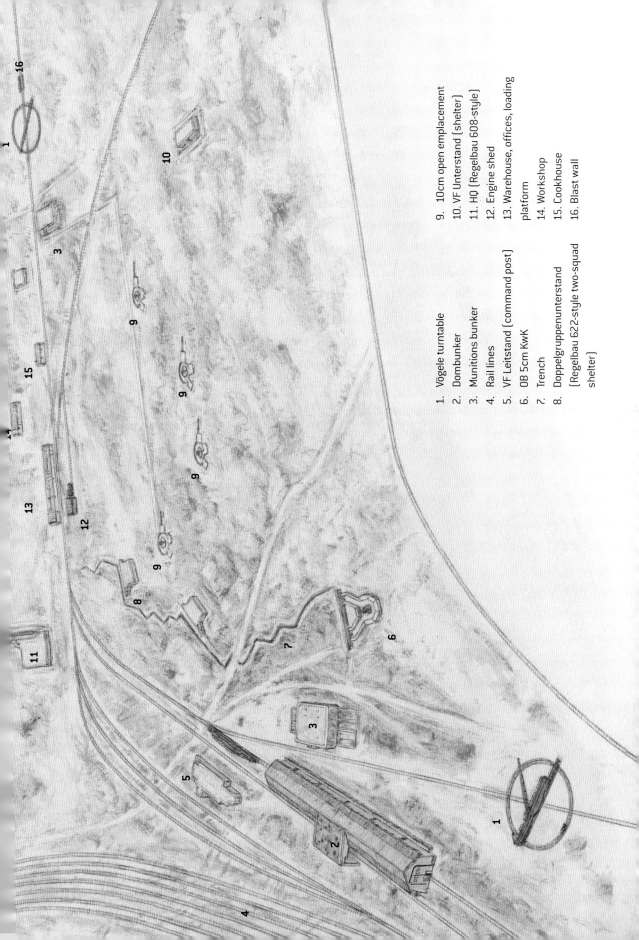

1. Vögele turntable
2. Dombunker
3. Munitions bunker
4. Rail lines
5. VF Leitstand (command post)
6. OB 5cm KwK
7. Trench
8. Doppelgruppenunterstand (Regelbau 622-style two-squad shelter)
9. 10cm open emplacement
10. VF Unterstand (shelter)
11. HQ (Regelbau 608-style)
12. Engine shed
13. Warehouse, offices, loading platform
14. Workshop
15. Cookhouse
16. Blast wall

```
                    ┌─────────────────────────┐
                    │  Festungspionierstab 27 │
                    │     Oberstleutnant K.   │
                    │        Michelmann       │
                    └─────────────────────────┘
```

| Abschnitt I Nieuport | Abschnitt II Calais | Abschnitt III Blanc Nez | Abschnitt IV Gris Nez* | Abschnitt V Boulogne | Abschnitt VI Marquise |

* Major T. von Heppe of Abschnitt IV was the only naval fortress engineer officer.
He was deployed in the construction of the battery 'Siegfried' ('Todt').

Festungspionierstab (Fortress Engineer Staff) 27.

by December 1940 Festungsbaustab Kanalküste – now Festungspionierstab (Fortress Engineer Staff) 27 – was split into six sections.

Festungspionierstab 27 covered the coast from Le Tréport to Bray-Dunes and had its headquarters at Hallines. It reported into Festungspionierkommandeur (Fortress Engineer Commander) XVIII who, in turn, reported to Inspekteur der Landesbefestigungen West (Inspector of the Land Fortifications West) and then to General der Pioniere und Festungen (General of Pioneers and Fortresses). Festungspionierkommandeur XVIII was allocated to Armee Oberkommando (AOK) 15 (15th Army HQ), which was established in January 1941 and was responsible for defending the Pas-de-Calais region.

The *Festungspioniere* structure in the West underwent a number of changes as the size and scale of the construction programme grew, especially around Calais, before work finally tailed off after D-Day in 1944.

SEEKOMMANDANT PAS-DE-CALAIS

Soon after the surrender of France, the Kriegsmarine, under Kommandierender Admiral Frankreich (Commanding Admiral France), took control of the coast. Immediately subordinate was the Marinebefehlshaber Kanalküste (Naval Headquarters Channel Coast), which was responsible for the coast in northern France and Belgium. In February 1941, this command was divided into four *Seekommandanten*. Later in

The Seekommandant Pas-de-Calais chain of command in December 1941.

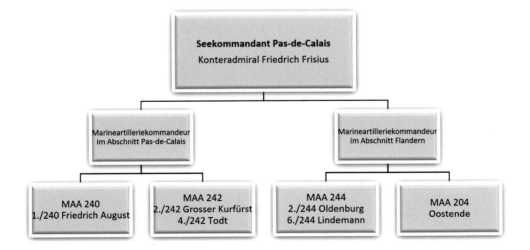

the year, these were dissolved and Seekommandant Pas-de-Calais was made responsible for this stretch of coast.

In July 1942, the Marineartilleriekommandeur im Abschnitt (Naval artillery commander for a section) roles were dissolved and the Marine-Artillerie-Abteilung (MAA – Naval artillery section) reported directly to Konteradmiral Frisius. These sections were responsible for the Marine-Küsten-Batterie (Naval coastal battery) including the cross-Channel guns. *Marine-Artillerie-Abteilungen* 240, 242 and 244 were formed in Lager Altengroden in May 1940, and following the defeat of France they were moved to the Pas-de-Calais. For the entirety of the war, MAA 240 was commanded by Korvettenkapitän M.A. der Reserve Fritz Diekmann and MAA 242 by Korvettenkapitän M.A. der Reserve Kurt Schilling. Both units were dissolved in September 1944. Marine-Artillerie-Abteilung 244 was initially commanded by Korvettenkapitän M.A. der Reserve Johannes Stührenberg (August 1940–May 1942). He was succeeded by Fregattenkapitän M.A. der Reserve Heinrich Garde (May 1942–October 1944), who commanded the unit until it was dissolved.

The cross-Channel guns were manned by officers, NCOs and men – see Table 7.

Table 7: German cross-Channel gun manpower complements					
	Year	*Offiziere* (officers)	*Unteroffiziere* (junior NCOs)	*Mannschaften* (men)	Total
Friedrich August	1941	2	30	102	134
	1943	1	36	206	243
Grosser Kurfürst		1	27	178	206
Lindemann	1942	4	41	445	490
	1943	4	34	280	318
Oldenburg	1941	4	15	181	200
	1942	8	30	175	213
	1943	3	34	138	175
Prinz Heinrich	1941	4	23	179	206
	1942	6	35	173	214
	1943	2	27	137	166
Todt	1943	4	49	337	390

Following the fall of France, the railway guns that had supported the blitzkrieg in the West were now deployed along the coast to bombard Britain as part of the preparations for Operation *Seelöwe*. Artillerie-Kommandeur 141 (Arko 141) was responsible for these guns.

Eisenbahn-Batterie 701 was established in the autumn of 1939 with a 21cm K12 V gun. After the defeat of France, the unit was moved to Wimereux and Bassin Carnot, Calais. In 1942, both K12s were deployed to Terlincthun, Boulogne before being moved to Hydrequent (Stützpunkt 192 'Bismarck') in January 1944.

Eisenbahn-Batterie 710 was established in September 1939 with two 28cm K5 guns. After the Western campaign, the battery was moved to Calais and fired against England for the first time on 28 August 1940. Later, the battery was housed at Fort Nieulay (Stützpunkt 89 'Fulda').

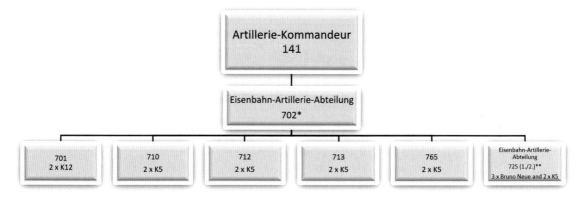

```
            Artillerie-Kommandeur
                     141

          Eisenbahn-Artillerie-Abteilung
                     702*

  701      710      712      713      765    Eisenbahn-Artillerie-
 2 x K12  2 x K5   2 x K5   2 x K5   2 x K5      Abteilung
                                              725 (1./2.)**
                                          3 x Bruno Neue and 2 x K5
```

* Later included Eisenbahn-Batterie 688.
** Abteilung 725 had two batteries: 1./725 and 2./725.

The organization of Artillerie-Kommandeur 141.

At Noirbernes, the Germans located two 28cm K5 rail guns. The position was furnished with Vögele turntables and SK ammunition bunkers – shown here. In the centre of the bunker the entrance can be seen. Inside there was an overhead rail for moving the shells from the ten compartments. This example has a Wellblech shelter attached (left). The official title of the position was Stützpunkt 180 'Schwarztal'. (Author's photograph)

Eisenbahn-Batterie 712 was established in August 1939 with two 28cm K5 guns. After the end of the Western campaign, the battery was located at Hydrequent until the start of 1944, when it was transferred to Italy (replaced by Eisenbahn-Batterie 701).

Eisenbahn-Batterie 713 was established in May 1940 with a 28cm K5 gun. After the defeat of France, the battery was deployed for coastal protection at Les Garennes. In August 1940, another 28cm K5 gun was assigned to the battery. In May 1941, the battery was moved east to be used in support of Operation *Barbarossa* but was soon transferred back to France to the area of AOK 15 (Ferme d'Inghen and Fréthun). In January 1944, the battery was moved to Noirbernes.

Eisenbahn-Batterie 765 was established in November 1940 with two 28cm K5 guns. In June 1941, it was deployed to the Eastern Front, but was then moved to the Channel coast near Noirbernes. At the end of 1943, it was moved to Fréthun.

Eisenbahn-Artillerie-Abteilung 725 was established in November 1940. After an initial deployment to the Eastern Front the unit moved to France. The first battery (1./725) was located at Coquelles cement works (Stützpunkt 124 'Bremen'). The second battery was positioned near Fréthun (Stützpunkt 113 'Uhu') before being deployed to Italy in September 1943.

Eisenbahn-Batterie 688 was formed in August 1939 with three 28cm 'Langer Bruno' guns. After the end of the Western campaign, the battery was assigned to coastal protection, but in March 1942, it was transferred to the Eastern Front. In November 1943, it returned to France newly equipped with two 28cm K5 guns and was placed under AOK 15 at Sangatte.

According to the *Kriegsstärkenachweisung* (theoretical composition) dated 15 July 1944, a railway battery with two 28cm K5 guns had a strength of five officers, 56 NCOs and 156 men.

ADOLF HITLER

Hitler had come to power in Germany in 1933, and one of his first actions was to consolidate his political control. He then started to reverse the restrictions imposed on Germany as part of the Paris peace settlement of 1919. He remilitarized the Rhineland, re-established an air-force and expanded the army and navy. Equally significantly, he also strengthened and extended the German border defences. He visited the East Wall in 1935 and again in 1938, but was underwhelmed by what he saw. The defences were massive, but lacked firepower. In July 1938, he ordered work to stop and all resources to be concentrated in the West on the West Wall.

Hitler's predilection for concrete defences seemed at odds with his advocacy of 'lightning warfare', but the western defences served to facilitate his grand ambitions in the east – securing his western border allowed him to concentrate his forces in the east to defeat the Bolsheviks and secure *Lebensraum* (living space). However, from his time serving on the Western Front in World War I, he was also very familiar with the devastating effect of artillery and the value of reinforced concrete to protect soldiers and their weapons.

With the fall of France, Hitler was able to combine these obsessions, and on 16 July 1940, he issued Führer Directive No. 16, which outlined preparations for a seaborne operation against England.

Among other things, the directive ordered that: 'Strong forces of coastal artillery must command and protect the forward coastal area.' More specifically, the navy was 'to coordinate the setting up of coastal artillery … The largest possible number of heavy guns will be brought into position as soon as possible in order to cover the crossing and to shield the flanks against enemy action at sea. For this purpose railway guns will also be used (reinforced by all available captured weapons) and will be sited on railway turntables. Those batteries intended only to deal with targets on the English mainland (K5 and K12) will not be included. Apart from this, the existing heavy gun batteries are to be enclosed in concrete opposite the Strait of Dover in such a manner that they can withstand the heaviest air attacks and will permanently, in all conditions, command the Strait of Dover within the limits of their range. The technical work will be the responsibility of the Organisation Todt.' The commanders-in-chief were to submit their plans, and for the Kriegsmarine this included, 'Details of the building of coastal batteries'.

As well as this Führer directive, Hitler also used the fortifications for propaganda purposes. In late December 1940, he took his special train to France and inspected the guns at Cap Gris-Nez. The visit was captured on film for domestic and overseas consumption.

Reich Minister Albert Speer, head of the Organisation Todt, visits the Atlantic Wall in 1943. Speer is inspecting the newly completed Batterie 'Lindemann', where each of the guns has now been protected by reinforced concrete shelters. (ullstein bild via Getty Images)

COMBAT

A little over two months after troops of the BEF landed back in Dover from the beaches around Dunkirk, the town, along with its near neighbours Folkestone and Deal, were hit by the first shells fired from German guns in France. Not that the people of Kent were aware of this at the time. On Monday 12 August, the peace of the coastal towns was shattered by a series of explosions. This was nothing new – Kent had been bombed by the Luftwaffe – but the skies were clear. A number of people were killed and houses destroyed. Later investigations established that these were the first victims of a silent killer – German railway guns located at Sangatte. Only ten days later, the Germans intensified the bombardment. On 22 August, the first fixed gun ('Grosser Kurfürst') shelled England. This brought an immediate response from across the Channel. Although the 14in. gun 'Winnie' was ready on 7 August, Churchill delayed its use until the Germans showed their hand. It now opened fire – the duel had begun in earnest.

Kent was shelled again in September and October and brought retaliatory fire from 'Winnie', but it was one against many, and despite support from the Royal Navy (HMS *Erebus* had shelled the coast at the end of September 1940) and the RAF, the British were not able to silence the German guns. To provide an element of protection for the civilian population, the authorities in Dover decided to introduce a special siren, but this distinctive double alert could only be used when shells had actually

A German 28cm K5 railway gun firing across the Channel on 19 November 1940. The gun is recorded as firing eight rounds that hit the area around St Margaret's at Cliffe, near Dover. (Sueddeutsche Zeitung Photo/ Alamy)

landed. It was introduced on 13 October and was first used on 18 October. Two days later, the Germans fired some 50 shells at the town. 'Winnie' was again ordered to respond. At the end of the shelling, the all clear was sounded. Residents emerged from their shelters to assess the damage, which was extensive, but casualties were thankfully few. The Germans soon modified their tactics to inflict maximum casualties. A newspaper reporter noted: 'One hour after the last shell the All Clear sounds. This does not mean that it is over. Jerry, knowing this, sometimes lobs another in, hoping to kill a few more people.' The reporter was John Steinbeck, author of the award-winning *The Grapes of Wrath*, who travelled to the UK to report on the war for the *New York Herald Tribune*.

As well as adapting their tactics, the Germans also adopted new munitions. On 1 November, the German guns again targeted Dover, but this was different from before with the Germans now also using airburst shells. In the following weeks, the shelling intensified. On 17 November, 45 shells were directed at the town; on 25 November, more than 100 shells were fired, with many aimed at the coastal batteries at St Margaret's; and on 28 November around 50 shells were fired. The British responded as best they could, with 'Winnie' firing three rounds at 'Grosser Kurfürst' on 17 November. However, analysis of the fall of shot identified that its performance was deteriorating, and the barrel was changed the following month. Unaware that 'Winnie' was out of action, the Germans continued their barrage and, in the first week of December, brought an early Christmas present to gunners stationed on the Dover breakwater with thousands of fish killed in the harbour.

It is clear from this that in the first months of the 'Battle for Britain' that this was not a duel in the dictionary sense – combat between two parties with matched weapons – because this was very one-sided. By comparison with the German salvoes, British shelling was perfunctory. In part this was due to the imbalance in numbers of long-range guns, but also the British were effectively firing blind. The gunners relied on air observation for feedback on the accuracy of their shelling and the Luftwaffe's

A view of HMS *Erebus* taken from HMS *Rodney* in 1940. The monitor was fitted with two 15in. guns, and in World War I had shelled the Belgium coast. Aware of her exploits, Churchill ordered the Royal Navy to fire on the German guns being installed in France. In September and October 1940, the monitor did shell the enemy coast, but not the German coastal batteries. (© Imperial War Museum, A197)

On 22 June 1942, the German 40.6cm guns 'Anton' and 'Bruno' of Batterie 'Lindemann' were test-fired. Here 'Anton' fires one of its massive shells towards England. The concrete casemate has still to be completed and the blast has destroyed some of the shuttering. (akg-images, AKG93872)

pre-eminence made this difficult, if not impossible. Observation from the UK mainland was possible in good weather but the facilities and equipment were very basic, comprising tables, wireless sets, telephones and wall maps.

In 1941, Hitler cancelled Operation *Seelöwe* and turned his attention to the Soviet Union. Troops and tanks were moved east along with rail guns that had been used to bombard Kent. The shelling of the south-east of England dropped off. At the same time, the British installed more coast batteries, with 'Pooh' and the South Foreland battery operational by the end of the year. The start of 1942 was equally uneventful until February, when the Kriegsmarine, supported by the Luftwaffe, and coastal batteries, launched Operation *Cerberus* – the Channel Dash.

THE CHANNEL DASH

In the period before the war, the Germans constructed a number of powerful warships designed to threaten British hegemony. These included iconic vessels such as the *Bismarck*, *Gneisenau*, *Graf Spee*, *Prinz Eugen*, *Scharnhorst* and *Tirpitz*.

The *Gneisenau* and her sister ship *Scharnhorst* were pocket battleships that had spent the early part of the war in the Atlantic targeting merchant vessels moving vital stores between North America and the UK. However, the demands of operating in a hostile environment like the Atlantic and the increased threat from the Royal Navy saw the battleships return to Brest for essential maintenance and resupply in March 1941. Their presence in the French port was noted by the British, and a number of bombing raids were launched. Both ships were damaged and had to go into dry dock.

Meanwhile, the newly commissioned battleship *Bismarck* and the heavy cruiser *Prinz Eugen* were sailing for the Atlantic, but were detected, and HMS *Hood*, the pride of the Royal Navy, and HMS *Prince of Wales* were dispatched to intercept them. HMS

SOUTH FORELAND BATTERY FIRING

In January 1942 work on South Foreland Battery was complete, and almost immediately the 9.2in. guns were in action as the Germans launched Operation *Cerberus* – the plan to move the capital ships *Gneisenau*, *Prinz Eugen* and *Scharnhorst* through the Strait of Dover to the relative safety of Germany. Though risky, the plan benefited from the element of surprise and also allowed the Luftwaffe to protect the armada. Moreover, the shorter days of winter and inclement weather would help cloak the operation. Nonetheless, the British were soon aware that something was afoot, and planes from the RAF and Fleet Air Arm were scrambled to engage the targets. By midday on 12 February 1942, the ships were heading towards the Strait of Dover.

Visibility was poor, but the coastal guns were readied to engage the targets. 'Winnie' and 'Pooh' had the range to hit the targets, but in the mirk were not capable of hitting moving targets, so it was all down to the men of 290th Coast Battery of 540th Coast Regiment at South Foreland.

Unable to observe the enemy ships, the gunners were relying on radar. An initial salvo was fired and the ships were seen to take evasive action on the screen, but no shell splashes were picked up that would have allowed the crew to re-calibrate their fire. In total, they fired 33 shells with three reported hits, but none were fatal. In spite of further air attacks and damage from mines, which slowed their progress, all of the ships made it through.

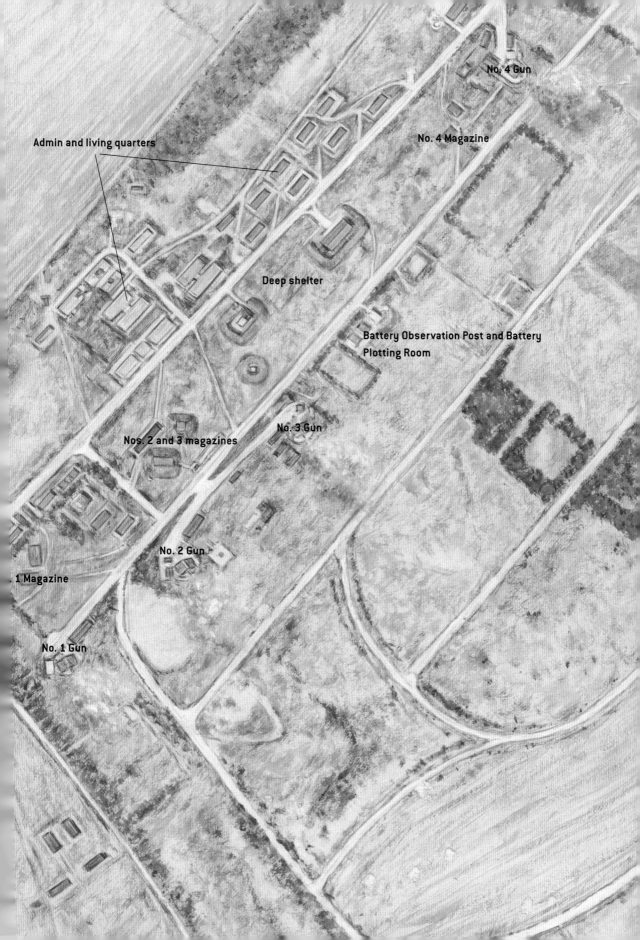

No. 4 Gun

No. 4 Magazine

Admin and living quarters

Deep shelter

Battery Observation Post and Battery Plotting Room

No. 3 Gun

Nos. 2 and 3 magazines

No. 2 Gun

1 Magazine

No. 1 Gun

Hood was sunk with the loss of 1,415 lives. The two German ships now headed for France, seeking a safe harbour and to undergo repairs, but *Bismarck* was torpedoed and on 27 May 1941 was sunk. *Prinz Eugen* escaped and on 1 June sailed into Brest. Six months later, the United States joined the war (7 December 1941) and the idea of capital ships attacking the convoys in the Atlantic was dropped; U-boats could undertake this task much more effectively. The *Gneisenau*, *Prinz Eugen* and *Scharnhorst* (together with the *Tirpitz*, already in Kiel) could be better employed attacking convoys heading for the Soviet Union. The problem was how to move three warships from Brest back to Germany without the British intercepting them. Both routes – via Iceland and through the English Channel – were fraught with danger. In the end, a decision was made to make a dash up the Channel. They would be protected by German destroyers and planes of the Luftwaffe commanded by Adolf Galland. The attempt would be made in the early months of 1942 to take advantage of the long winter nights and inclement weather. And to improve the chances of success, the British radar was jammed.

On the night of 11 February 1942, Hitler ordered the Kriegsmarine to launch Operation *Cerberus*. Maintaining complete radio silence, the three ships left Brest and through good luck and incompetence were not spotted until lunchtime on 12 February. By this time, the ships were approaching the narrowest point of the Channel. The British radar spotted the group and the guns around Dover were primed. However, 'Winnie' and 'Pooh' had a slow rate of fire and were not capable of engaging moving targets, so could do little to interdict the convoy. The onus thus fell on the newly installed 9.2in. guns of the South Foreland battery. Visibility was poor (5 nautical miles) and no one could get visuals on the enemy ships, which were hugging the French coast. The guns would have to aim using radar, but the enemy ships were zig-zagging and it was nigh on impossible to identify the *Gneisenau*, *Prinz Eugen* and *Scharnhorst* from the radar blips. The guns opened fire at 12.19, but neither radar nor binoculars could identify the fall of fire. The crews of the ships, by contrast, could see the gun flashes and the shells fall harmlessly into the Channel well astern. E-boats made smoke to further disguise the convoy. Two more salvoes were fired, but again it was impossible to see the fall of fire and there was no further explosion to suggest a hit. The battery continued to fire, but was now targeted by enemy long-range guns, with one shell falling on the perimeter wire. There was no damage or casualties, but South Foreland suspended operations. The battery history recorded that: 'Independent observation from RAF and RN give at least three hits.' British destroyers and torpedo boats and bombers, both traditional and armed with torpedoes, now engaged the convoy, but they were similarly ineffectual. Only mines sown in the Channel achieved any success, with both the *Gneisenau* and *Scharnhorst* falling victim. Though damaged, they still managed to make it to Germany. Hitler was exultant, and Churchill was incandescent with rage at the inability of his forces to stop this audacious escape.

***

As the Germans advanced into the Soviet Union, the rail guns, unable to use the rail lines because they were a different gauge, were redeployed back to France, and in the summer of 1942 the cross-Channel shelling intensified. On 12/13 August 1942, South Foreland loosed off 54 rounds at a hostile convoy. This brought a response from the German guns, with shelling between Dover and St Margaret's over several days. On 14 and 15 August, South Foreland was in action again, engaging a German convoy. The 76 rounds were answered with 17 from the other side of the Channel on 15 August, with one salvo hitting Langdon battery.

After the disastrous Dieppe raid on 19 August 1942, shelling recommenced on 6 September with South Foreland firing 68 rounds at an enemy convoy. The German response in the evening was devastating, with over 100 shells hitting the area to the east of Dover.

On 9 November, South Foreland fired a record number of shells – 140. But this landmark brought a swift and deadly

reaction. Gun flashes on the French coast were observed, and minutes later Dover was hit, as was Folkestone with seven shells finding their target, killing two and injuring 18 others. On 11 November, a searchlight battery near Folkestone was hit killing four soldiers. The following day, more gun flashes were observed and again Folkestone was hit, but there were no casualties. The intensive shelling saw the introduction of a new warning signal for the town and a change of barrels for the battery at South Foreland. They were back in action in early December and on 10–11 December they fired 92 rounds. The Germans responded by shelling Dover and Folkestone, killing three.

The shorter days and reduced visibility meant that 1943 started quietly, but the increased use of radar meant that guns on both sides of the Channel could fire without direct observation of the target. On 10 February, South Foreland fired 93 rounds at a target in the Channel. In response to the British shelling, the guns at Wanstone were targeted by the enemy and a gunner from 540 Coast Regiment was killed as was Edith Burvill, who worked at the Fan Bay NAAFI. A little under a month later, on 2–3 March, radar was used by the South Foreland battery to identify and engage enemy targets in the Channel. The four guns fired 177 rounds, with five confirmed hits. The Germans responded hitting Folkestone and Dover, sinking HM Trawler *Opossum*, which was alongside. A little over a week later, South Foreland engaged a large merchant vessel, with escort ships, that was observed leaving Boulogne harbour. Motor torpedo boats (MTBs) and motor gun boats (MGBs) were also deployed in this combined-arms operation. In an effort to suppress the British fire, German guns shelled the Dover area. On 5 April, another German convoy and its escort vessels were spotted on radar. 'Jane' and 'Clem' fired 75 rounds with 13 confirmed hits and one enemy vessel sunk. The German long-range guns fired on Dover and Folkestone, killing two.

On 28 June 1943, the Dover Coastal Force flotilla spotted a large German convoy near the French coast. Although unable to hit the enemy vessels, the 6in. guns at Fan Bay opened fire. Seeing the gun flashes the ships took evasive action and adopted a zig-zag pattern familiar to British plotters, who were now able to estimate the course and range of each vessel. Coordinates were passed to Wanstone and South Foreland batteries, which shelled the hapless targets for an hour. Disappointingly for the British gunners, only a single hit was recorded before the German guns responded.

One of the small tractors pulling a trailer with ammunition for either 'Jane' or 'Clem'. Just to the rear is the entrance to the magazine. This was constructed from brick, and above are camouflaged nets. The photograph was taken on 17 September 1944 when the Wanstone battery was supporting the Canadian ground assault in France. (Library and Archives Canada/Department of National Defence, e011504670)

This piece of armour was taken from the gun shield of the 40.6cm gun Cäsar, which was part of Batterie 'Lindemann'. It shows the shells that were fired at England. However, it understates the true number, because it does not show those shells fired after D-Day in June 1944. The message says '*Es flogen gegen Engeland*' – literally, 'They flew against England'. The plate has been installed on Dover seafront. (Author's photograph)

The trick was repeated by the British gunners on 3 October, and on the following day the Wanstone and South Foreland batteries engaged a German convoy sinking one with a further two seen to beach. The Germans responded targeting Dover and Folkestone, but the shelling was less heavy.

In January 1944, the last air raids on Dover took place, but the shells continued to fall. On 20 January, a German vessel was targeted by the 15in. guns at Wanstone. The RAF reconnoitred the site and identified the 7,000-ton MV *Walkenried* (previously the MV *Munsterland*) off Sangatte already sinking. The PM sent an effusive note to the Commander Coast Artillery, congratulating him on the good shooting. On 20 March 1944, the Wanstone and South Foreland batteries hit and sank the 4,000-ton naval tanker SS *Rekum* (ironically built in Glasgow). The enemy responded by firing 20 shells at Dover, killing four.

On D-Day, the Germans shelled ships in the Channel and hit SS *Sambut*, and on the following day they shelled Dover, killing three – though for some reason they did not target sections of the Mulberry Harbour being towed down the Channel to Normandy. A week after D-Day, the first V-1 flying bomb was spotted, but the shelling continued – and on the same day, Folkestone endured its heaviest bombardment, with 42 shells hitting the town in a five-hour onslaught that caused widespread damage.

Through the summer, the south-east and the capital were targeted with V-1s. However, once their launch sites had been overrun, this menace was extinguished, only to be replaced by heavier and more frequent shelling. On 1 September, Deal was shelled for five hours. On the same day, Ramsgate and Margate were hit, causing considerable damage, killing two and injuring 17 – thankfully these were the last shells to hit the district.[1] Folkestone was hit by eight shells and 26 shells hit Dover, killing eight.

---

1 Broadstairs, Margate and Ramsgate had all been targeted by the enemy's guns. The latter bore the brunt, with 42 shells hitting the town. The first shells hit Ramsgate in February 1941. The intensity increased in 1943 with 27 shells hitting the district, killing eight people.

Across the Channel there was similar carnage. As the Canadians approached the port of Boulogne, the Germans tried to evacuate the vessels marooned in the port. On 1–2 September, some 40 vessels slipped anchor, including *Sperrbrechers* (minefield pathfinders) and *Räumboote* (R-boats, or minesweepers), and made for safer harbours. Radar picked up the movement, and South Foreland fired 122 shells, sinking 11 vessels (and probably three more). This precipitated significant counter-battery fire, with 14 shells hitting South Foreland, and was answered by shelling from Wanstone. A couple of days later (4–5 September), six E-boats left Boulogne and were also engaged by South Foreland. The four guns fired 85 shells, hitting one of the E-boats, which were reported as moving at high speed (40 knots). This was the last major action of South Foreland. In that same action, 'Jane' and 'Clem' shelled the German coastal batteries. 'Bruno', one of the guns of Batterie 'Lindemann', was disabled; later, a shell was put in the chamber to destroy it.

A picture of Clarence Street in Folkestone after it had been hit by shells on 9 November 1942. Seven shells were fired at the town from Batterie 'Todt,' one of which hit Clarence Street, killing two people and injuring 18. (Kent Archives)

The advance of the Canadians and the very real threat of being overrun prompted the German batteries to loose off the rounds sitting in their magazines. Folkestone experienced its heaviest shelling since 1940, with 64 shells hitting the town in the month. The costliest day was 14 September, when approximately 20 shells hit the town, killing six people. The intensity of the shelling eased, and on 25 September, the last shells hit. Folkestone had been shelled 36 times and hit 218 times, killing 32.

Nor did Dover escape the death throes of the German cross-Channel guns. Despite everything that had gone before, the shelling in September was described as being the worst that Dover had experienced. The town was shelled almost every day, killing 62 people. Though the Canadians were closing in, the Germans continued to fire, and on 25 September killed six people in the town. The following day, the last day of shelling, the Germans fired 50 shells, killing seven.

The unluckiest victim was perhaps Patience Ransley. She had made her way to one of the deep underground shelters for protection. One of the shells from Batterie 'Lindemann' exploded a few feet above the reinforced concrete roof of the tunnel. The blast destroyed the roof and killed the 63-year-old. Though little consolation for those who had died or been injured, Sergeant Duncan of the Canadian Scottish Regiment sent a flag to the people of Dover that they had captured from the last cross-Channel gun at Cap Gris-Nez.

John Steinbeck wrote about the shelling of Dover and in 1958 published *Once There Was a War*. He wrote: 'The Dover man has taken perhaps a little more pounding than most, not in great blitzes, but in every-day bombing and shelling, and still he is not impressed … Surveying a building wrecked by a big shell, he says, "Jerry was bad last night," as he would discuss a windstorm.'

Troops of the North Shore Regiment examining 'Cäsar', one of the 40.6cm guns of Batterie 'Lindemann' on 26 September 1944. The position has been damaged by Allied bombs/shells, but remains operational. The soldiers give a sense of the scale of the gun and the casemate. (Donald I. Grant/Library and Archives Canada/Department of National Defence, PA133143)

THE CHANNEL PORTS

In June 1944, the Allies landed in Normandy; the first step in liberating occupied Europe from German rule. After consolidating the beachhead, advances were slow. However, at the end of July the Allies broke out and quickly pushed the German forces back. Paris was liberated on 25 August, and less than a month later the Allies had reached the German border. The Canadians, who had fought their way ashore at Juno beach, were given the important but less than glamourous task of securing the Channel ports in what became known as the 'Cinderella campaign'. This was made all the more challenging by the fact that at the start of September, Hitler declared the Channel ports to be 'fortresses' – defended to the last man. In meeting their strategic objective, the Canadians also necessarily had to roll up much of the Atlantic Wall, including the cross-Channel guns at Cap Gris-Nez and Blanc-Nez.

Although the Americans had secured the port of Cherbourg, and the Mulberry harbour was operational, the Allies still needed a deep-water port. Accordingly, the First Canadian Army was tasked with capturing Le Havre and silencing the battery at Grand Clos (1 x 380mm gun and 2 x 170 guns). They were supported by HMS *Erebus*, reprising its earlier exploits, but the monitor was hit by German fire and withdrew. On 10 September, *Erebus* and HMS *Warspite* targeted the German guns again, along with air support, and this time they put the guns out of action. With Le Havre captured, the Canadians were ordered to advance on Antwerp. Boulogne,

HMS *EREBUS* FIRING ON FRENCH COAST

In August 1940, Churchill asked about the possibility of HMS *Erebus*, a monitor commissioned in 1916, being used to destroy or at least disrupt the construction of German gun batteries around Calais. The Navy was receptive to the idea. However, for Vice Admiral Ramsay, CinC Dover, the more immediate threat comprised the barges that were being assembled at Calais ready for an invasion of the British Isles. He planned to target these, and only if this proved impossible was *Erebus* to engage the German coastal batteries. The operation was planned for 28 September 1940, but was aborted and was reorganized for the following day. This time *Erebus* made it to its assigned location in the Channel. In the early hours of 30 September, *Erebus* opened fire on Calais with its two 15in. guns, but only managed to fire 17 rounds before she had to return to port.

Despite these setbacks, a plan was developed for a further operation to target the guns at Cap Gris-Nez in the first week of October. This was again delayed, and then the plan was changed – the target was now the docks at Dunkirk. After a false start on 11 October, the operation was successfully completed on 16 October with 50 shells hitting the target. Through the winter, operations were suspended, but in February 1941 *Erebus* was again deployed in the Channel to target Ostend (repeating her exploits of World War I). Fifty-four shells were fired, but did no serious damage. The plan for the Royal Navy to attack German forces on the coast was now suspended, though not dropped. On D-Day, *Erebus* provided fire support, targeting German gun batteries near Utah Beach.

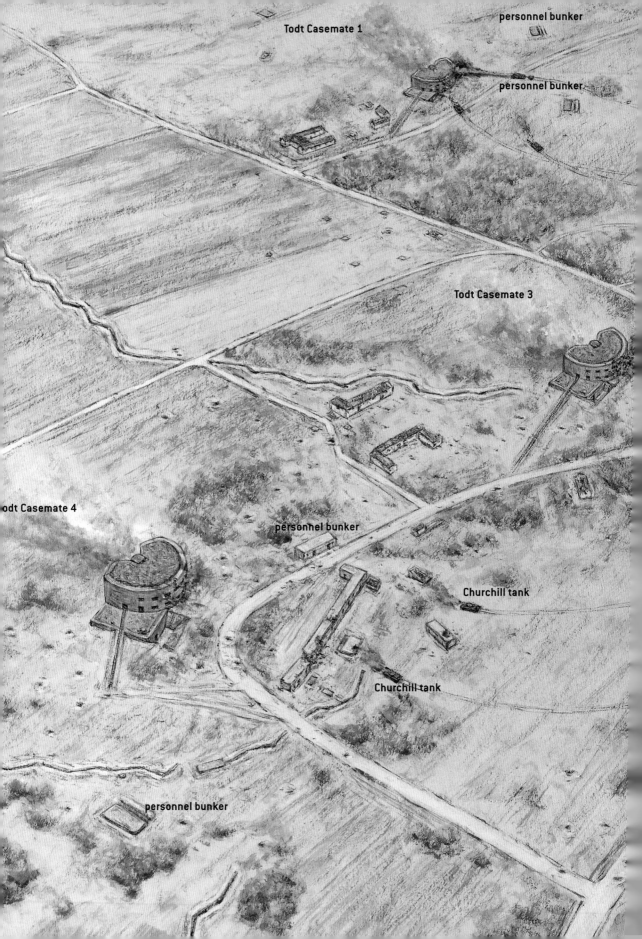

personnel bunker

Todt Casemate 1

personnel bunker

Todt Casemate 3

Todt Casemate 4

personnel bunker

Churchill tank

Churchill tank

personnel bunker

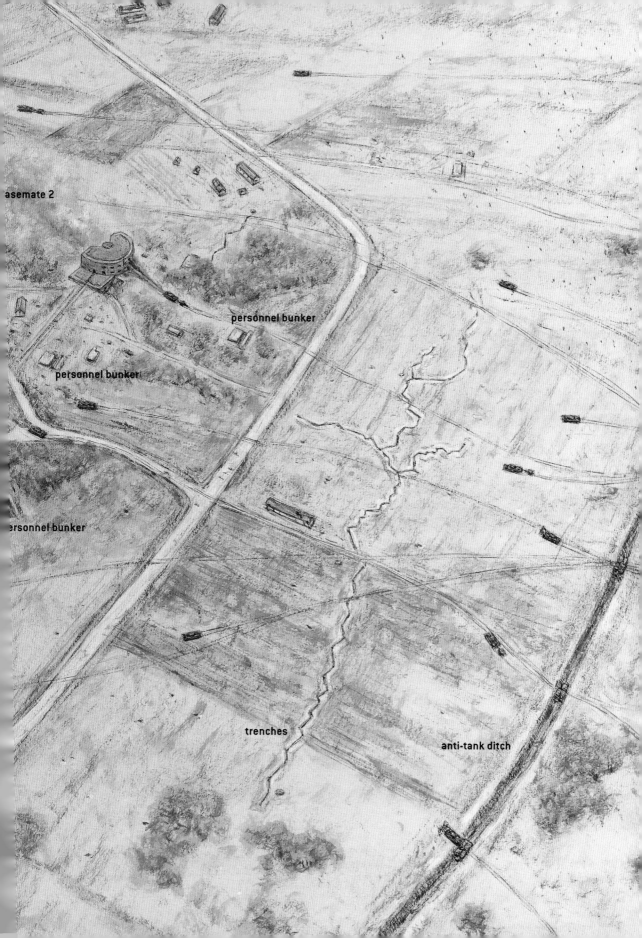

asemate 2

personnel bunker

personnel bunker

personnel bunker

trenches

anti-tank ditch

On 29 September 1944, the North Nova Scotia Highlanders (Novas) and the Highland Light Infantry (HLI) of Canada of 9th Canadian Infantry Brigade attacked the German positions on Cap Gris-Nez. The HLI on the right was to attack towards Framzelle and capture Batterie 'Grosser Kurfürst', while the Novas on the left were to strike towards Haringzelles and capture Batterie 'Todt'. The 38cm guns of Batterie 'Todt' could not rotate to target an attack from the rear, but the landward approach had been protected with an anti-tank ditch, barbed wire and mines. Prior to the attack, the German positions were softened up by Allied bombing and artillery. At 06.45, AVREs of 141st Regiment RAC led the attack dropping fascines into ditches to allow flail tanks to move forward and clear the minefields. The Novas, supported by Churchill flamethrower tanks, and the AVREs armed with petards, advanced with B Company on the left and D Company on the right. D Company quickly overran No. 1 casemate on the far right. B Company now engaged the other three huge casemates. Churchills armed with petards attacked No. 3 casemate. These explosive charges had limited effect on the thick concrete. More effective were the exploits of Lieutenant Fitch's platoon, who managed to get a soldier on the roof of a casemate and dropped grenades down the vent, which was enough to convince the garrison to surrender. Eventually, the crews of all the casemates surrendered. On the right flank, the HLI was similarly successful capturing 'Grosser Kurfürst' and reaching the coast.

Calais and Dunkirk were considered of secondary importance, and if they proved too difficult to capture, they would be sealed off and left for later.

Lead elements of 3rd Canadian Infantry Division reached Boulogne on 3 September and began to reconnoitre the defences. They concluded that they were strong and extensive – Hitler had recognized the importance of the port and already in January 1944 had declared it a 'fortress'. To capture the port, the Canadians would need to prepare and launch a set-piece attack with air support and artillery. This was not immediately available because it was all being utilized in the operation to capture Le Havre. Consequently, the attack had to be delayed. The capture of Boulogne – Operation *Wellhit* – was set for 17 September.

As with the operation to secure Le Havre, the Canadians recognized the need to suppress or eliminate the fire from large-calibre German coastal guns. (Batterie 'Grosser Kurfürst', with its 360-degree traverse, had already targeted Allied units; its 28cm shells were known to the Canadians as 'freight trains'.) Thus, 'The Brigadier Royal Artillery, First Canadian Army [Brigadier H.O.N. Brownfield] flew to England and arranged for the mammoth guns on the South Foreland east of Dover to fire on the German cross-Channel batteries in the Calais–Cap Gris-Nez area, to prevent them from interfering with the attack on Boulogne'. Ranging shots were fired on 16 September. Air observation provided feedback on the fall of shells, and on 17 September the 'German battery positions were hit repeatedly; and one of the 15in. guns scored a direct hit on one of the 16-inchers of the great German Noires Mottes battery ['Lindemann'] near Sangatte … The 15in. guns fired until their old barrels were so worn that they could no longer reach the French coast. The 14in. ['Winnie' and 'Pooh'] were in action again on 19 and 20 September'.[2]

The operation to capture Boulogne also included capturing the 30.5cm guns of Batterie 'Friedrich August' at La Trésorerie. This attack was to be conducted by troops of the North Shore (New Brunswick) Regiment. Their first objective was the Pas de Gay feature which dominated the battlefield. From here the New Brunswickers would have a perfect view of the naval guns. On 18 September, following a short bombardment, the regiment attacked. The defenders were determined, and it was not until the following day that the position was secured. Unlike the operation to secure Le Havre, the attack was delivered without naval support, and the official Canadian history questions whether this was because of the threat posed by the heavy gun batteries around Calais.

The German garrison in Boulogne finally surrendered on 22 September 1944, but to utilize the port, the Allies needed to neutralize the heavy gun batteries around Calais and Cap Gris-Nez. The 3rd Canadian Infantry Division was given the job of leading the attack – Operation *Undergo*. Lead elements of the division had already reached Calais by 5 September and the Regina Rifles had captured the four 150mm guns at Wissant. This prompted Major-General Spry, commander of 3rd Canadian Infantry Division, to try to rush the positions on Cap Gris-Nez. On 16–17 September, 7th Canadian Infantry Brigade attacked the gun batteries, but the endeavour failed. Again, it was realized that the position was held in strength and would need a set-piece attack.

2   Colonel C.P. Stacey, *Official History of the Canadian Army in the Second World War*, Vol. III: *The Victory Campaign*, The Queen's Printer and Controller of Stationery, Ottawa, 1960, pp. 338–39.

A rare colour view of the 15in guns of Wanstone Battery firing in September 1944. In the foreground are the Harco ventilators on top of the ammunition store. The extensive use of camouflage netting is clear. Just visible in the background is the South Foreland Lighthouse. (Library and Archives Canada/Department of National Defence, e010786328)

Though smaller than Boulogne, Calais was a valuable port. For many years, it had been an English possession and had been besieged numerous times. The fortifications were old, but would be difficult to overcome, the more so because since mid-August the Germans had undertaken work to protect the landward approaches, including flooding large areas. On 25 September, the Canadians launched Operation *Undergo*. To protect Canadian forces attacking Calais, a massive smokescreen was laid to ensure that the 28cm guns of Batterie 'Grosser Kurfürst' could not be used against them.

At the same time, a subsidiary attack was launched against Cap Blanc-Nez. On the morning of 25 September, 8th Canadian Infantry Brigade advanced. The Régiment de la Chaudière captured the Cap, and at first light on the following day the North Shore Regiment captured the 40.6cm guns of Batterie 'Lindemann'.

At Cap Gris-Nez, batteries 'Todt' and 'Grosser Kurfürst' were still in German hands. As the Canadians approached the big guns, the shelling of Kent intensified. It was therefore imperative that these positions were captured and silenced. The job was given to 9th Canadian Infantry Brigade. To suppress enemy fire and further demoralize the crews, the RAF bombed the Cap, firstly on 26 September, and then on 28 September when 855 tons of bombs were dropped.

On the following day, the North Nova Scotia Highlanders attacked Batterie 'Todt' and captured the position. To the north, the Highland Light Infantry (HLI) of Canada attacked Batterie 'Grosser Kurfürst'. By 10.30 – just four hours after the supporting artillery had opened fire – the HLI had captured the guns. However, one gun continued to operate even though enemy troops were on the turret. It fired 'one shell wildly out to sea, another in the direction of Dover and one more inland before sappers could put it out of action with hand-placed charges'.[3]

In the fighting to silence the cross-Channel guns and secure the nearby ports, the Allies suffered heavy losses. At the Commonwealth War Graves Commission cemetery at Leubringhen, France there are 729 burials. Of these, 594 are Canadians who lost their lives in the period 5–30 September 1944. (Author's photograph)

3   Stacey 1960, p. 353

ANALYSIS

When considering the performance of the long-range guns deployed on either side of the Channel, it is important to remember that, with a couple of notable exceptions (the German K12 and K5 rail guns) the ordnance was old – some dating to before World War I. The barrels had often been provided by the navy and repurposed as either railway guns or coastal artillery. Age was not the only challenge. The effectiveness of the long-range guns was also affected by the ability of the crew to identify, track and then hit a target. Gun laying had not evolved appreciably since World War I, with both sides relying on direct observation either from the ground or the air. At night, or in poor weather, the ability to fire accurately was difficult, if not impossible. Only later did radar make any meaningful contribution.

The rudimentary nature of the fire control was not critical for the rail guns, which had limited traverse and relied on indirect fire. In 1940, the Germans were quick to deploy their K12 and K5 rail guns to shell Britain. Suitable sections of track were identified to enable them to hit towns in Kent which were large and whose location was already known. Later, Vögele turntables and 'T' rail sections were utilized, which enabled the rail guns to traverse, but not quickly enough to engage moving targets – a fact exacerbated by the slow rate of fire. On the other side of the Channel, the British also deployed rail guns. However,

The Dombunker for a rail gun at Stützpunkt 89 'Fulda', Calais Nieulay. This was made from reinforced concrete and was cigar-shaped. The entrance would have been protected by large steel doors. To the left is an SK ammunition bunker. Behind these two positions was a Vögele turntable, which allowed the rail gun to traverse. (Author's photograph)

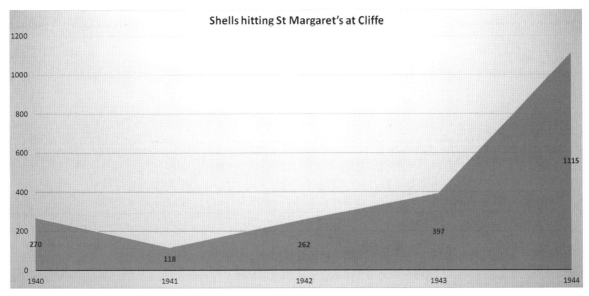

Shells hitting St Margaret's at Cliffe

270 — 1940
118 — 1941
262 — 1942
397 — 1943
1115 — 1944

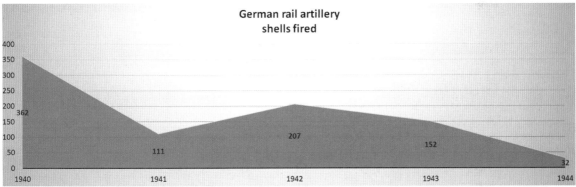

German rail artillery shells fired

362 — 1940
111 — 1941
207 — 1942
152 — 1943
32 — 1944

the smaller-calibre guns (12in. and below) did not have the range to hit France. Somewhat surprisingly, the largest of the British rail guns – HMG 'Boche Buster' – was also incapable of clearing the Channel. The 13.5in. rail guns ('Gladiator', 'Piecemaker' and 'Scene Shifter') with a supercharge could fire around 37km – just far enough to reach France, but at the extremes of their range were not accurate.

To supplement the rail guns, both sides installed fixed coastal batteries. For the Germans, these guns were deployed to dominate the Channel and provide long-range artillery support for an invading army. Hundreds of shells were fired at Kent in 1940 in preparation for an invasion. However, in October 1940 the plan to invade Britain was postponed, and in the following year Hitler invaded the Soviet Union; rail guns were moved east and the shelling of south-east England eased. This is clearly shown in the graph 'German rail artillery shells fired'. In the succeeding years, the intensity of the shelling increased, especially from German coastal batteries, with population centres again targeted. The graph 'Shells hitting St Margaret's at Cliffe' shows the shelling of the sea-side town and gives a sense of how the attacks ramped up. The damage and casualties caused by the shelling was significant. Dover was particularly badly hit.

Table 8: Dover damage			
	Dover	Dover rural district	Total
German shells	2,284	719	3,003
Casualties			
Killed	199 (107)*	5	204
Seriously injured	307 (200)*	10	317
Slightly injured	420 (221)*	8	428
Damage to property			
Destroyed	910	36	946
Severely damaged	2,998	141	3,139
Slightly damaged	7,135	1,942	9,077

Source: *Kent: The County Administration in War 1939–45*, Kent County Council, 1946.

* The number in brackets is from the *Dover Express* and relates directly to shells. Other deaths and injuries were from bombing (HE, oil and incendiary as well as flying bombs).

Shells for use by 'Pooh' have been moved to the gun position and are stored under camouflage netting on wooden beams with chocks holding them in place. Gunners can be seen manhandling one of the 14in. shells on to a trolley that runs on a narrow-gauge railway. The crew then push the trolley to the gun. Just visible in the foreground is the full-gauge rail line. (Library and Archives Canada/Department of National Defence, e011504662)

COUNTER-BATTERY FIRE

In spite of careful camouflaging and the creation of dummy gun positions, German aerial reconnaissance of the British coast identified a number of gun sites under construction. When these batteries had been completed and started to fire, the Germans retaliated and specifically targeted these guns. Fire was directed against South Foreland on a number of occasions from the summer of 1942. Initially, there were no injuries, and there was only slight damage to the Battery Observation Post (BOP), the NAAFI (a recreational facility), cookhouse, stores and officers' and sergeants' messes. However, in 1944 the intensity of the counter-battery fire increased. In March, No. 2 gun was damaged, as was the Fan Bay battery. Then, on 1–2 September, South Foreland was hit by 14 shells. No. 2 gun was put out of action and there were six casualties.

British guns also targeted their German counterparts to try to silence them. When South Foreland came under fire at the start of September 1944, the Wanstone battery responded in turn. Later in the month, the British guns were in action again. In a final irony, the guns installed to deter a German invasion were now used to target their German counterparts as the victorious Allies advanced towards Germany. 'Winnie', 'Pooh', 'Jane' and 'Clem', with aerial observation provided by an Auster, fired on batteries 'Todt' and 'Lindemann', damaging the latter. However, the damage was mostly superficial and the batteries continued to fire until they surrendered to the Canadians days later.

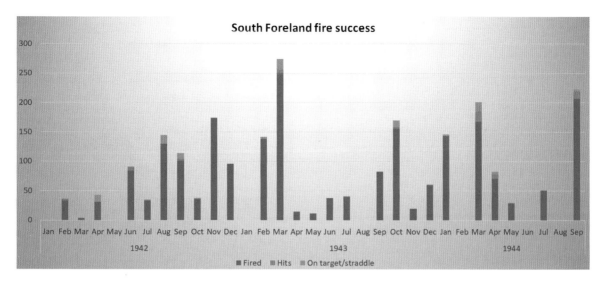

South Foreland fire success

Fired ■ Hits ■ On target/straddle

SHIPPING

Both the British and the Germans also targeted shipping in the Channel. Shore-based guns on fixed mounts were significantly more accurate than guns mounted on naval vessels, but this operation was still difficult, in part because of the reliance on direct observation, but there were also other factors:

- At longer ranges, the trajectory of the shell was not flat, which meant that even if the point of impact had been correctly calculated, the shot could go over or fall short of the target.
- The shell had to fly a considerable distance, which meant that the target, seeing a gun flash, could take evasive action.
- As barrels wore out, performance diminished, which made it more difficult to hit the target. (The South Foreland guns were replaced on four occasions during the war: November/early December 1942; May/June 1943; mid-March 1944; and again just before D-Day.)

To improve the performance of their coastal batteries, the British introduced new technology, adapted their tactics and embraced combined arms operations.

At the start of 1942, the four 9.2in. guns at South Foreland were ready for action. Almost immediately, in February 1942, they were in use, firing on the German capital ships in their audacious Channel Dash. They fired 33 shells, but weather conditions were poor and only three hits were confirmed. These were the first of more than 2,000 shells fired by the battery in the period to the end of September 1944. Analysis of the records suggests that the percentage of hits (or on target/straddles) was initially relatively low. (It was not always possible to confirm hits/on target, and as such records detailing coastal batteries' performance are not perfect.) However, increasingly, the British made use of radar to both identify ships and to map the fall of shot. Even in poor visibility, this enabled them to adjust their fire and target enemy vessels. From the spring of 1943 onwards, radar was increasingly used and provided much better bearing and range discrimination, and performance did improve. The graph 'South Foreland fire success' gives a sense of this.

The increasing use of radar also coincided with the adoption of new tactics by both sides. To respond to the increasing threat posed by the coastal guns around Dover, the Germans developed countermeasures. Based on gun flashes/fall of shot, German vessels would take evasive action or would slow down/speed up. This was initially successful, but the Allied gunners introduced the so-called 'Turning Procedure'. When a target was identified, the smaller guns of Fan Bay would open fire. They did not necessarily have the range to hit the target, but at distance the flash was indistinguishable from the larger-calibre guns and would elicit evasive action from the target. This had been carefully observed by the British in previous months and based on this analysis, the bigger guns would be ordered to fire on the target's expected bearing. This was used to good effect – in total 28 vessels were sunk.

Other enemy vessels were attacked by the Royal Navy. In July 1943, Operation *Dusty* was introduced. When an enemy vessel was identified, coastal gun batteries would engage the targets. Meanwhile, small navy craft (MTBs or MGBs) were dispatched to intercept. As the boats closed on their target, with the enemy distracted by incoming shells, the batteries would cease fire and the motor boats would attack. This was undoubtedly successful, but frustrated the gunners who were understandably disgruntled when ordered to disengage and miss out on a potential 'kill'.

The Germans also targeted enemy shipping, but with limited success. The reason for this is not immediately discernible, because they had radar and the large-calibre guns were manned by naval personnel. One notable success was scored on D-Day when the SS *Sambut*, a government-owned Liberty ship loaded with troops and equipment destined for Normandy, was hit by German coastal guns. Four crew and a number of troops are known to have died when the ship was sunk. Later, on 24 June 1944, the *Empire Lough*, loaded with 2,800 tons of petrol, set sail from London as part of a larger convoy (ETC-17, made up of 21 coastal vessels protected by the corvette HMS *Sunflower*, fresh from supporting Operation *Neptune*, and the Lend-Lease frigate HMS *Dakins*) destined for Normandy. As it transited the Channel, it was hit by German shells and set on fire. The master managed to beach the vessel, but he died, as did another member of the crew. The vessel was lost. The freighter *Gurden Gates* was also damaged in the same engagement, but was later repaired.

The SS *Sambut* ablaze after being hit by shells fired by Batterie 'Todt' and Batterie 'Lindemann' on 6 June 1944. *Sambut* was a liberty ship built in 1943 that was heading from Southend-on-Sea to Normandy loaded with troops and equipment. Four of the crew were killed in the attack.

(www.wrecksite.eu)

AFTERMATH

In the UK after World War II there was a great sense of optimism and a desire to move forward. In Dover, where almost half of the town's houses were destroyed or damaged by bombing or shelling, prefabricated buildings were erected to provide temporary accommodation. More concrete, in all senses of the word, was the fate of Marine Parade, which had been badly damaged. It was demolished and replaced with the Gateway Flats complex – brutalist architecture that divided opinion then as now.

This desire to dispense with the old and embrace the new was not conducive to the preservation of war relics. The first guns to be installed – 'Winnie' and 'Pooh' – were the first to be dismantled. Worn out after the heavy shelling in September 1944, they were scrapped at the end of the war. (At least one 14in. gun still exists and is currently on display at the Royal Armouries Museum, Fort Nelson, Hampshire, UK.) The other coastal batteries were maintained for a time, but were slowly wound down. In 1947, South Foreland No. 4 gun was moved to Plymouth (Renny Battery) and the rest of the battery was decommissioned when coastal defence was dissolved in 1956. In 1957, 'Jane' was cut up by Dover Industries Ltd and was front-page news in the *Dover Express*. The only 15in. guns left are outside the Imperial War Museum, London.

The story of the British gun batteries since then is somewhat mixed. All the guns have been removed, but some remnants of 'Bruce' remain, though the area is heavily overgrown. South Foreland is on public land and munition stores, gun bases and the BOP can be seen; fences ensure that public safety is maintained. Numerous detailed signs have been provided by the White Cliffs Countryside Partnership, so that visitors get a sense of what was there. 'Clem' and 'Jane' are on land owned by the National Trust and although access is currently restricted, work has started to restore the site, including the nearby AA position. (Fan Bay is also owned by the National Trust and is open to the public.) However, the sites of 'Winnie' and 'Pooh' have fared less well. After the guns were removed, the infrastructure was largely demolished and the site levelled. Now little can be found on the ground, save for some of the magazines, which provide shelter for cows. An excavation was made of the site of 'Winnie' in 2003 as part of a television series – *Two Men in a Trench* – which uncovered some remains, but the trench was backfilled. Away from the guns, Dover Museum has a good section on the town's role in the war including the

Very little remains today of the 14in. gun position 'Winnie'. The gun was removed and the site was backfilled. At the entrance to the field where 'Winnie' was located are a number of ammunition stores. These had a thick concrete roof and brick-faced walls. Steel doors secured the room. Visible on the ceiling are the remnants of the shell hoist. (Author's photograph)

A view of 'Jane' taken from the top of No. 2 ammunition store. To the left it is just possible to see the gun position and the power plant. In the centre is an open space where two Nissen huts were located for the gun crew. In the rear right of the photo is the other ammunition store with brick entranceway. (Author's photograph courtesy of National Trust)

cross-Channel guns. Dover Castle, which is managed by English Heritage, is open to the public and covers the 2,000 years of history on the site and includes the role played by the castle in World War II.

Sadly, the British rail guns have not survived. Even before the end of the war, they had been removed from the coast. Consideration was given to employing rail guns in the invasion of occupied Europe, but ground-attack aircraft like the Typhoon were so effective that the idea was shelved. The 13.5in. guns were scrapped in 1945 and 'Boche Buster' in 1947. An 18in. gun is on display at the Royal Armouries Museum, Fort Nelson.

The remains of Turret 4 of Batterie 'Grosser Kurfürst'. The main gun positions were destroyed after the war by British engineers. The 28cm gun has gone, but you can still see the remains of the S412 shelter. The curve of the gun pit on the right is clearly visible. (Author's photograph)

Ironically, on the other side of the Channel the defences which saw heavy fighting and bombing are in a reasonable state of repair. This is in part down to the huge quantities of reinforced concrete used, which resisted not only Allied attack but also post-war efforts to demolish them. (Batterie 'Prinz Heinrich' was moved to Leningrad in 1943, but some bunkers remain.) 'Oldenburg' is still in a very good state of preservation and for a long time individuals could gain access, but more recently this area was used by migrants and the bunkers have all been sealed. Development of the site near La Trésorerie, Boulogne-sur-Mer means

that much of Batterie 'Friedrich August' has gone, but one casemate still remains. All of Batterie 'Todt' has survived and one of the casemates has been transformed into an excellent museum – Musée du Mur de l'Atlantique. 'Grosser Kurfürst' was less fortunate. It was destroyed after the war by the Royal Engineers. However, the most egregious loss is Batterie 'Lindemann'. This was the largest of the cross-Channel gun batteries, but it was decided that the waste from the Channel Tunnel would be dumped on the site and as such little is left to be seen of these positions. A section of armoured plate taken from Batterie 'Lindemann' is displayed on Dover front.

Part of the V-3 complex at Mimoyecques was demolished by the British after the war. The complex was later used as a mushroom farm before opening as a museum in 1984 – Forteresse de Mimoyecques.

Most of the German rail guns were destroyed as Hitler's forces retreated, and others were captured. One of them, the K5 Leopold, is on display at the Musée du Mur de l'Atlantique. Some of the sites that housed the rail guns have survived including the bunkers at Noirbernes, and a number of the reinforced concrete Dombunkers that protected the rail guns. However, all of them are on private land.

The remains of these massive German guns provide a sobering reminder of this small, but sanguinary struggle. Thousands of shells were fired by both sides, countless lives were lost and the damage was extensive. However, the duel has been largely overlooked in the history books. Hopefully, this title goes some way to redress this balance.

GLOSSARY

AA	Anti-aircraft
AP	Armour-piercing
APHE	Armour-piercing high-explosive
Artillerie Kommandeur	Artillery commander
AVRE	Armoured Vehicle Royal Engineers
BC	Battery Commander
Betonbettung	Concrete foundation
Bettungsgeschütz	Gun on a platform mounting
Bettungsschiessgerüst (BSG)	Platform firing framework
BL	Breech loading (gun)
BOP	Battery Observation Post from where fire is directed by the BC
BPR	Battery Plotting Room
Bty	Battery, a sub unit of a regiment of artillery usually commanded by a major
CA	Coast Artillery
CCCA	Commander Corps Coast Artillery
CCRA	Commander Corps Royal Artillery
CD	Coast Defence
CHL	Chain Home Low
CO	Commanding Officer
CRA	Commander Royal Artillery

Einsatz	Deployment
Eisenbahnartillerie	Railway artillery
Eisenbahn-Artillerie-Abteilung	Railway artillery section
Eisenbahn und Bettungsgeschütz	Railway and platform mounted gun
FC	Fire Command
Festungsbaustab	Fortress Construction Staff
Festungspionier (kommandeur)	Fortress Engineer (Commander)
Festungspionierstab	Fortress Engineer Staff
FOP	Forward Observation Post
FPR	Fortress Plotting Room
Geschützbrunnen	Circular concrete gun pits
Gruppenunterstand	Squad shelter or bunker
HE	High-explosive
Kanone Eisenbahn K (E)	Rail gun
Kasematte	Casemate
Kriegsstärkenachweisung (K.St.N)	German documents that showed the theoretical composition of a unit
Küsten-Drehscheiben-Lafette (Kst.Drh.L)	Coastal turntable mount, generally for a turret
L – Länge (in Kaliber)	Length (in calibre)
Leitstand	Fire control bunker
Marine-Artillerie-Abteilung (MAA)	Naval artillery section
Marinebau-Bataillon	Naval Construction Battalion
Marinebefehlshaber	Naval Headquarters
Marine-Küsten-Batterie (MKB)	Navy Coast Battery
MGB	Motor gun boat
MTB	Motor torpedo boat
Munitionsunterstand	Ammunition shelter or bunker
NAAFI	Navy, Army and Air Force Institutes
RA	Royal Artillery
RCA	The Royal Regiment of Canadian Artillery
RE	Royal Engineers
Regelbau (R)	Standard design bunker identified by unique number or moniker
RGA	Royal Garrison Artillery
RM	Royal Marines
SK	Schnelladekanone – quick-loading cannon, or Schiffskanone – ship cannon. See note below.
Sperrbrecher	German auxiliary ship with reinforced hull that cleared routes for other vessels through minefields
Stützpunkt	Strongpoint
TA	Territorial Army
Vergeltungswaffe	Vengeance Weapon

Note: German naval gun designations changed in the first half of the 20th century. In the period before and during World War I, German guns were designated by their bore diameter in centimetres, SK (meaning ship cannon), and their calibre. So, for example, 30.5cm SK L/50. L refers to length in calibre. In the period between 1920 and 1940, the calibre length figure was dropped and replaced by the year of construction. For example, the 38cm SK C/34 is a ship's cannon firing a 38cm shell that was designed in 1934.

BIBLIOGRAPHY

Arnold, Colonel B., *Conflict Across the Strait* (Crabwell and Buckland Publications, Dover, 1982)

Chazette, A., *Les Batteries Cotieres en France Vol. I, II, III* (Editions Histoire et Fortifications, France, 2004, 2005)

Chazette, A., *Les Batteries Cotieres du Nord – Pas-de-Calais* (Editions Histoire et Fortifications, France, 2006)

Chazette, A., *La Batterie Lindemann* (Editions Histoire et Fortifications, France, 2014)

Collyer, D.G., *Deal & District at War* (The History Press, Stroud, 2009)

Dobinson, C., *Twentieth Century Fortifications in England Vol. VI.1 Coast Artillery* (Council for British Archaeology, York, 2000)

Engelmann, J., *German Railroad Guns in Action – Armor No.15* (Squadron Signal Publications Inc., Texas, 1976)

Ford, K., *Run the Gauntlet: The Channel Dash 1942*, Raid series no. 28 (Osprey Publishing, Oxford, 2012)

Forwood, M., *The Elham Valley Railway* (Phillimore, London, 1975)

Gander, T.J. and Chamberlain, P., *Small Arms, Artillery and Special Weapons of the Third Reich* (Macdonald and Jane's Publishers Ltd., London, 1978)

Gückelhorn, W. and Paul, D., *Eisenbahnartillerie: Einsatzgeschichte der deutschen Eisenbahnartillerie im Westen 1940 bis 1945* (Helios Verlags, Aachen, 2014)

Hart, B., *The Elham Valley Line 1887–1947* (Wild Swan Publications, Berkshire, 1984)

Hart, B., *The Elham Valley Railway* (Wild Swan Books Ltd., Bath, 2015)

Hogg, I.V., *Coast Defences of England and Wales 1856–1956* (David & Charles, London, 1974)

Hogg, I.V., *German Artillery of World War 2* (Arms and Armour Press, London, 1975)

Hogg, I.V., *British and American Artillery of World War 2* (Arms and Armour Press, London, 1978)

Humphreys, R., *Target Folkestone* (Meresborough Books, Rainham, 1990)

Humphreys, R., *Thanet at War 1939–45* (Alan Sutton Publishing Ltd., Stroud, 1991)

Humphreys, R., *Dover at War 1939–45* (Alan Sutton Publishing Ltd., Stroud, 1993)

Humphreys, R., *Hellfire Corner: Reminiscences of Wartime in South-East England* (Alan Sutton Publishing Ltd., Stroud, 1994)

Lyne, R., *Military Railways in Kent* (North Kent Books, Maidstone, 1983)

Maurice-Jones, Colonel K., *The History of Coast Artillery in the British Army* (The Naval and Military Press Ltd., Uckfield, 2005)

Olejniczak, H., *Le Mur de L'Atlantique dans la Baie de Wissant* (Imprimerie Barnéoud, Bonchamp-les-Laval, 2009)

Sakkers, H. and Machielse, M., *Artillerieduell der Fernkampfgeschütze am Pas-de-Calais 1940–1944* (Helios Verlags, Aachen, 2013)

Stacey, Colonel C.P., *Official History of the Canadian Army in the Second World War*, Vol. III: *The Victory Campaign* (The Queen's Printer and Controller of Stationery, Ottawa, 1960)

Wilcox, D., *Army Radar: The Story of its Development and Employment in World War II* (Reveille Press, Brighton, 2014)

Zaloga, S.J., *German V Weapon Sites 1943–45*, Fortress series no. 72 (Osprey Publishing, Oxford, 2008)

Zaloga, S.J., *Railway Guns of World War II*, New Vanguard series no. 231 (Osprey Publishing, Oxford, 2016)

Zaloga, S.J., *Superguns 1854–1991*, New Vanguard series no. 265 (Osprey Publishing, Oxford, 2018)

Articles

Brown, M. and Pattison, P., 'Western Heights Dover, Kent – Report No.8', *Archaeological Investigation Report Series*, 29/2001 (English Heritage, 2003)

Gander, T., '28cm Railway Gun at Calais', *After the Battle* No. 78

Gander, T., 'Twentieth Century British Coast Defence Guns', *Fortlet* No. 2 (2011)

Reed, J., 'The Cross Channel Guns', *After the Battle* No. 29

Sencicle, L., 'Dover's Home Guard', *The Dover Historian* (2016)

INDEX